Mary Page
Peter Guthrie
Sloan Sable

Rules of the Game 3

EDUCATORS PUBLISHING SERVICE
Cambridge and Toronto

Printed in U.S.A
ISBN 0-8388-2241-X
978-0-8388-2241-8

19 PPG 21

CONTENTS

INTRODUCTION

In *Rules of the Game* we set out to write a grammar series that would encourage students to discover that grammar is just another name for the patterns that exist in language. In our own teaching, we have discovered that students learn grammar more effectively if they can, in some sense, recreate the process by which rules and definitions have evolved. To achieve this goal, we start each lesson with examples and directed questions, clues to help students see that rules and definitions begin with language and are not handed down from some invisible legislature.

The exercises that follow each lesson rely on both traditional and not-so-traditional approaches. As in most grammar books, we give students sentences and ask them to pick out various points of grammar; but as often as possible we also provide opportunities for students to respond more creatively, using what they have learned. For example, students may be asked to follow sentence patterns, write their own sentences, choose effective modifiers, or combine sentences. Teachers can assign all exercises at the time a concept is introduced, assign the identification problems to diagnose weaknesses, or even save some exercises for those occasions when specific problems occur in student writing.

The lessons are arranged in a way that has worked well with our students. Frequently lessons build on each other: the lesson on the compound sentence appears not long after students have learned what constitutes a sentence and right after they have been introduced to the conjunction. Teachers should feel free, however, to skip around or to supplement in areas where students need more follow-up work. The comprehensive exercises may be used to supplement, to diagnose, or to evaluate.

We hope this series begins a discovery for students that will end only when they can use clear, correct, and effective language to express their ideas.

PART I. REVIEW

1. FUNCTIONS OF THE NOUN

SUBJECT: The subject of a sentence is the noun or pronoun that is doing the action of the verb. Subjects and verbs are the building blocks of sentences.

S
<u>Roberta</u> was graduated from medical school ten years ago.

DIRECT OBJECT: A direct object is a noun or pronoun that receives the action of its verb.

DO
Roberta treats many <u>people</u> during an average day.

INDIRECT OBJECT: An indirect object is a noun or pronoun that indirectly receives, or is affected by, the action of a verb.

IO
Roberta always gives her <u>patients</u> her full attention.

PREDICATE NOUN or PREDICATE NOMINATIVE: A predicate noun is a noun or pronoun that comes after a linking verb and renames or identifies the subject.

PN
Today Roberta is an experienced <u>doctor</u>.

APPOSITIVE: An appositive is a noun or pronoun that comes directly after another noun or pronoun and renames that noun or pronoun.

APP
Roberta shares her office with another doctor, <u>Paula Wong</u>.

OBJECT OF THE PREPOSITION: An object of a preposition is a noun or pronoun that appears at the end of a prepositional phrase. The preposition connects it to the rest of the sentence.

OP
Roberta's office is located in a big <u>city</u>.

PREDICATE ADJECTIVE: A predicate adjective is an adjective that comes after a linking verb and describes or limits the subject.

PA   PA
Roberta is <u>happy</u> and <u>successful</u>.

A. *Directions:* Write the function* of the underlined noun or pronoun in the space provided at the end of each sentence. If the underlined word is a predicate adjective, write "predicate adjective" in the space.

EXAMPLE: <u>Hester</u> ate her dinner. _____subject_____

1. Mr. Springer, my <u>teacher</u>, was absent. _____
2. My little brother broke my <u>radio</u>. _____
3. The <u>desert</u> can be a beautiful place. _____
4. Jenny blew out the <u>candles</u> on her cake. _____
5. She seemed an old <u>woman</u> after her accident.

   _____

6. Eric appeared very <u>tired</u> after the game. _____
7. Elizabeth wrote a <u>report</u> about whales. _____
8. Alan is a superb chess <u>player</u>. _____
9. He ate two boxes of <u>popcorn</u> at the movie. _____
10. <u>Yesterday</u> was the coldest day of the year. _____
11. She read <u>them</u> an Inuit folk tale. _____
12. Julia handed him the note after <u>school</u>. _____
13. <u>We</u> lost the game in overtime. _____
14. My gerbil, <u>Derby</u>, loves sunflower seeds. _____
15. Folk music is <u>popular</u> with all kinds of people.

    _____

16. Gregory's boss gave <u>him</u> an excellent recommendation.

    _____

17. <u>It</u> rained all day without stopping. _____
18. July is often the hottest <u>month</u> of the year. _____
19. Why did you come to <u>class</u> so late? _____
20. They presented the <u>committee</u> their demands.

    _____

---

*Subject, Direct Object, Indirect Object, Predicate Noun, Predicate Adjective, Appositive, Object of the Preposition

B. *Directions:* Label the function of each underlined noun or pronoun in the following sentences. Label predicate adjectives, too.

S for subject
DO for direct object
IO for indirect object
OP for object of the preposition

PN for predicate noun
APP for appositive
PA for predicate adjective

EXAMPLE: $\overset{\text{S}}{\underline{\text{Heather}}}$ left without her $\overset{\text{OP}}{\underline{\text{book}}}$.

THE LOST CONTINENT OF ATLANTIS

1. Atlantis is a legendary lost <u>continent</u> in the <u>Atlantic Ocean</u>.
2. <u>It</u> was first mentioned by the Athenian philosopher, <u>Plato</u>.
3. In his <u>tale</u>, Atlantis was an <u>empire</u> of ten kingdoms.
4. The <u>people</u> of Atlantis were <u>powerful</u> and wealthy.
5. Eventually <u>they</u> conquered other <u>lands</u> in the area.
6. The people of <u>Athens</u> resisted their <u>attacks</u> and defeated them.
7. The gods punished <u>Atlantis</u> for its wars against its <u>neighbors</u>.
8. They sent <u>it</u> violent earthquakes and <u>floods</u>.
9. <u>Atlantis</u> sank beneath the <u>sea</u> in a single day and a night.
10. Supposedly, these <u>events</u> occurred 9,000 years before the rule of the Athenian statesman, <u>Solon</u>.
11. Plato provided future <u>generations</u> a compelling <u>tale</u> of mystery and adventure.
12. All kinds of people, <u>archaeologists</u>, geologists, and mystics, have investigated the ''<u>truth</u>'' about the lost island.
13. The numerous <u>theories</u> about Atlantis are often <u>fanciful</u>.
14. According to one, the biblical <u>paradise</u>, <u>Eden</u>, was located there.
15. According to another, the Indian <u>colonists</u> of the great pre-Columbian <u>civilizations</u> came from this land.
16. Oceanographers discovered a Minoan <u>city</u> on the Greek island, <u>Thira</u>.
17. <u>Thira</u> was buried by volcanic ash in <u>1500</u> B.C.
18. Perhaps <u>it</u> was <u>part</u> of the lost civilization of Atlantis.
19. The legend of Atlantis has given many <u>writers</u> <u>inspiration</u>.

20. The submerged continent is a <u>subject</u> of Jules Verne's *Twenty Thousand Leagues Under the Sea*.

C. *Directions:* Underline the nouns and pronouns in the following sentences. (Don't underline possessive pronouns.) Then label the function of each of these nouns and pronouns. Also, underline and label any predicate adjectives.

S for subject	PN for predicate noun
DO for direct object	APP for appositive
IO for indirect object	PA for predicate adjective
OP for object of the preposition	

EXAMPLE:
<pre>
          S   DO   OP
</pre>
<u>Robert</u> ate his <u>dinner</u> in the <u>kitchen</u>.

1. The members of the school band were excited about their performance.
2. Her grandmother sent her a beautiful gift.
3. Florence, a skillful gymnast, got the highest score.
4. Roger is a good math student, but he was confused today.
5. The tour provided us information about colonial America.
6. Rebecca played her favorite piece, a Schubert Impromptu.
7. Where did Alfonso ever get that ridiculous hat?
8. I searched the house everywhere and never found my keys.
9. Sarah's hamster is tiny and cute.
10. The phone rang, and no one answered it.
11. My daughter has an extensive collection of fossils.
12. He promised his teacher an outline of his paper by Monday.
13. At her party they showed *Wait Until Dark*, a very scary movie.
14. My friend is an excellent swimmer, but she hates diving.
15. My brother, Billy, made me a copy of my favorite tape.
16. How could you lose your jacket in the middle of the winter?
17. The newspaper deliverer always brings us the paper late.
18. The grocery store was a madhouse before Thanksgiving.
19. The coach put ice on Juan's sprained ankle.
20. The director of the play, my father, did not give me a big part.

D. *Directions:* Each of the following problems indicates a particular function of the noun or pronoun. Make up sentences of your own that contain the indicated functions. Then underline the word that functions in that manner.

EXAMPLE: direct object

Judy ate a chocolate-covered <u>ant</u>.

1. object of the preposition

_____

2. appositive

_____

3. predicate adjective

_____

4. predicate noun

_____

5. appositive

_____

6. indirect object

_____

7. predicate noun

_____

8. direct object

_____

9. object of the preposition

_____

10. subject

_____

2. PARTS OF SPEECH

NOUN: A **noun** is a word that names a person, animal, place, thing, idea, or feeling.

The <u>unicorn</u> gave us <u>companionship</u>.

PRONOUN: A **pronoun** is a word that takes the place of a noun.

<u>He</u> wrote down <u>her</u> assignments. <u>She</u> likes small cars because <u>they</u> use less gas.

VERB: A **verb** is a word that expresses an action or a state of being.

The old man <u>was</u> tired, so his grandson <u>ran</u> ahead.

ADJECTIVE: An **adjective** is a word that describes or limits a noun or pronoun by telling which one, what kind, or how many.*

The guide saw the <u>grassy</u> plain.

ADVERB: An **adverb** is a word that describes or limits a verb, adjective, or other adverb and answers the questions, *How? When? Where?* or *To what extent?***

Jessica read the book <u>very thoroughly</u>.

PREPOSITION: A **preposition** is a word that joins or shows a relationship between a noun or pronoun and some other word in the sentence.

(<u>Without</u> a doubt), you are the silliest boy (<u>in</u> the class).

INTERJECTION: An **interjection** is a word that expresses a strong or sudden emotion and has no grammatical relationship with other words in the sentence.

<u>Drat</u>! That cat has eaten the fish again.

CONJUNCTION: A **conjunction** is a word that joins words or groups of words of equal rank.

<u>Either</u> you <u>or</u> your brother will make the beds <u>and</u> sweep the floor.

---

*Sometimes nouns and pronouns function, or work, as adjectives in a sentence.
  <u>Myra's</u> bag fell off <u>her</u> desk.
**Sometimes nouns function as adverbs.
  We took the hamster <u>home</u>.

A. *Directions:* Write the abbreviation for the correct part of speech above each of the underlined words in the following sentences. If a noun functions as either an adjective or adverb, label it according to its function.

N for noun	ADV for adverb
PRO for pronoun	PREP for preposition
V for verb	CONJ for conjunction
ADJ for adjective	INT for interjection

                       V   N
EXAMPLE: Jennifer <u>kicked</u> the <u>ball</u> hard.

1. Emily <u>won</u> the <u>raffle</u> <u>at</u> the auction.
2. <u>She</u> got a <u>giant</u> python <u>and</u> a bicycle for her birthday.
3. <u>Ben</u> <u>was</u> very excited about <u>his</u> project.
4. Jed's <u>soccer</u> shoes were <u>completely</u> destroyed by his <u>new</u> puppy.
5. <u>They</u> were absolutely stunned <u>by</u> her <u>announcement</u>.
6. Louisa was <u>not</u> pleased <u>with</u> her dessert and <u>refused</u> to eat it.
7. Philip loves his new <u>coach</u>, but he <u>also</u> misses his <u>old</u> one.
8. The <u>Arabian</u> stallion ran swiftly <u>across</u> the <u>field</u>.
9. The <u>hike</u> <u>was</u> very difficult <u>in</u> the rain.
10. Their <u>ski</u> trip was very successful, <u>but</u> they arrived home <u>late</u>.
11. The ball landed in the <u>neighbor's</u> <u>yard</u> and <u>then</u> rolled into the pond.
12. The baseball game lasted until after <u>dark</u>, and <u>no</u> one <u>could</u> <u>see</u> the ball.
13. <u>She</u> was <u>breathless</u> and could not finish the <u>grueling</u> race.
14. The <u>Civil War</u> ended in <u>1865</u>, but the issues dividing the country lasted <u>longer</u>.
15. *Invasion of the Body Snatchers* <u>is</u> a frightening movie <u>about</u> giant pea pods.
16. <u>Soon</u> she <u>will need</u> <u>a</u> larger violin.
17. Clyde <u>quickly</u> gulped down his breakfast <u>and</u> left <u>immediately</u> for school.
18. <u>My</u> schedule is <u>very</u> heavy <u>this</u> week.
19. <u>Help</u>! I left <u>Jane's</u> costume <u>on</u> the bus.

20. <u>Some</u> tourists are afraid of heights, <u>so</u> they <u>never</u> climb to the tops of the pyramids in Egypt.

B. *Directions:* Label the part of speech of every word in the following sentences. If a noun functions as either an adjective or adverb, label it according to its function. You do not have to label articles.

PRO for noun	ADV for adverb
PRO for pronoun	PREP for preposition
V for verb	CONJ for conjunction
ADJ for adjective	INT for interjection

```
         PRO V  ADV PREP   ADJ     N
EXAMPLE: I  sat down on  a broken chair.
```

YELLOWSTONE NATIONAL PARK

1. Yellowstone became our first and largest national park in 1872.
2. It is located in the northwest corner of Wyoming.
3. Men have been living there since the last ice age.
4. The first white man in Yellowstone was John Colter.
5. He came and trapped animals there in 1807.
6. Alas! Forty years later the scarcity of furs brought trapping to an end.
7. Soon a new type of exploration began.
8. It was based on curiosity.
9. Few believed the bizarre tales about this strange land.
10. Men talked of boiling-hot water that jetted 180 feet out of the earth.
11. Today the geyser Old Faithful is well known.
12. A geyser acts like a pressure cooker on a kitchen stove.
13. Deep in the earth boiling water produces steam.
14. Eventually, enough steam accumulates, and an explosion occurs that throws forth jets of heated water and steam.
15. Yellowstone also has many other fabulous attractions.
16. There are hot springs, canyons, rivers, lakes, and unbelievable wildlife.
17. Grizzly and brown bears, elk, and bison roam through the park.

18. Wait! Do not get too close to them.

19. They may seem cute and gentle, but they can be dangerous.

20. With all these attractions Yellowstone is our most popular national park.

3. SENTENCES

SENTENCE: A **sentence** is a group of words that contains a subject and a verb and expresses a complete thought. In its most basic form this complete thought is called an **independent clause** or **simple sentence**.

World War II began in 1940.

SENTENCE FRAGMENT: A **sentence fragment** is a group of words that does not express a complete thought. Sentence fragments do not finish the ideas or thoughts they begin; they leave you hanging.

Whether you believe it or not.

RUN-ON SENTENCE: A **run-on sentence** consists of two or more sentences that are linked together without the correct punctuation.

I like peanut butter, it is my favorite food.*

COMPOUND SENTENCE: A **compound sentence** consists of two or more simple sentences (independent clauses) joined by a coordinating conjunction.

Plants take in carbon dioxide, and they give off oxygen.

A. *Directions:* In the space at the end of each group of words, write **F** if it is a fragment, **R** if it is a run-on, and **S** if it is a sentence.
EXAMPLE: Yes, over there. __F__

1. The talent show beginning with a ventriloquist. _____
2. Without a doubt traffic will be heavy, we will leave early.

   _____
3. Whatever you decide. _____
4. Cranberries one of the main agricultural products of Cape Cod, Massachusetts. _____
5. On account of the blowing winds, freezing temperatures, and heavily falling precipitation. _____

---

*The correct way to write this sentence is as *two* sentences: I like peanut butter. It is my favorite food.

6. Standing under the arbor with his hat in hand. ____

7. On behalf of the entire class, Mary Ellen accepted the prize, she had been the chairperson and had coordinated the fund drive. ____

8. Andrew Wyeth, the son of the well-known illustrator N.C. Wyeth, the father of the painter Jamie Wyeth, and a famous painter himself. ____

9. A small religious group known as the Shakers. ____

10. Beside the fountain stood the man, thin and dark. ____

11. Herman Melville, an American author, writing *Moby Dick* despite critical attacks. ____

12. Laurence Olivier started acting in school at the age of ten, after seventy years of acting he was one of the world's best-known Shakespearean actors. ____

13. There are many. ____

14. Everybody helped to finish the work. ____

15. After Emily Bronte wrote *Wuthering Heights*. ____

16. Inspired by an evening of hearing and telling ghost stories, Mary Shelley wrote the novel *Frankenstein* from start to finish in one night. ____

17. The Red Baron having flown many successful missions for Germany and having survived many "dog fights" with other planes during World War I. ____

18. Because of the students' interest in the battlefield sites of the Civil War. ____

19. Sam Shepard, seen in movies such as *Country* and *Crimes of the Heart*, is a respected playwright. ____

20. Where after school? ____

B. *Directions:* Revise the following groups of words into one or two complete sentences. You may have to add words, capitalize letters, and change or insert punctuation.
   EXAMPLE: After Luis left the store
            After Luis left the store, he carried the groceries home.

1. Before the airplane landed

   _____

2. The first electric vacuum cleaner was patented in 1901, by 1927 vacuum cleaners were in more than half of the electrified homes in America _____

_____

3. Watching football every Sunday _____

_____

4. In the Middle Ages town dwellers used the main rooms of their houses for many purposes, cooking, sleeping, eating, and conducting business all happened in the same room. _____

_____

5. Outraged by the insensitive treatment _____

_____

6. The cottage near the jetty on the beach _____

_____

7. Thomas Hardy trained as an architect, consequently, in his novels he often gives precise and vivid descriptions of buildings. ____

_____

8. Although I take the bus to school in the morning _____

_____

9. Beatrix Potter spent many years writing books for children, however writing was not her only career. _____

_____

10. Whenever Josie goes skateboarding _____

_____

11. The wrestling team excited by the upcoming vacation _____

_____

12. Before the twentieth century smoking was restricted in large houses to smoking rooms now smoking is restricted or prohibited in many public places _____

_____

13. Underneath the dirty socks in the locker _____

_____

14. Housed in the Smithsonian, the Hope Diamond _____

_____

15. Since the faucet sprang a leak _____

_____

C. *Directions:* Depending on what type of sentence it is, write **simple** or **compound** in the space provided after each of the following sentences.
EXAMPLE: I love Lucy and Ethel. _____simple_____

1. Janet and Michael spent time with Jack's sons.

    _____

2. Please take notes on the following: character, setting, and atmosphere. _____

3. Whitney visited Houston with her mother, Cissy, and then went on to Dallas and Brownsville. _____

4. Paul felt like a new man after exercise. _____

5. The wheelchair participants began the marathon before the runners, and the crowd cheered them on. _____

6. When will you be arriving in Tucson, and when do you think your luggage will arrive? _____

7. The class will go to Sturbridge Village on Monday, or they will go to Plimouth Plantation on Friday. _____

8. Stevie plays a woodwind instrument in the school orchestra, but his friend plays a percussion instrument. _____

9. Bono saw me in detention and asked, "You, too?"

    _____

10. Mr. Soto outlined the rules, and we listened.

    _____

11. During the ride to school, Mrs. Gibbons asked her son about his report card. _____

12. Every night Gladys peeled an orange, but she didn't remove the pips. _____

13. On vacation Stewart always took his rod and reel to the lake.

    _____

14. During the game Eric clapped and whistled loudly; the fans yelled cheers. _____

15. Why are there so many stories about mythical kingdoms?

    _____

16. Ice skaters spend hours practicing their routines; precision is essential in competition.   _____

17. Starfish can regenerate from limbs, and for many years oyster fishermen cut up starfish and unwittingly created more of them.

    _____

18. Sand bars appear at low tide and expose the eggs of crabs to their main predator, the seagull.   _____

19. Samantha arrived early at school, for she wanted to run laps before classes.   _____

20. Pouring rain frequently obscures the driver's vision.

    _____

4. PUNCTUATION

END PUNCTUATION: **End punctuation** signals the end of a sentence. Periods, question marks, and exclamation points are the three types of end punctuation. Periods are used at the end of statements (declarative sentences). They are also used at the end of commands (imperative sentences) and indirect questions. Question marks are used at the end of questions (interrogative sentences). Exclamation points are used at the end of exclamations (words or sentences that express strong or sudden feeling).

Where is he going?
He is going to the carnival.
I told him not to go!

COMMA: **Commas**, which are used either alone or in pairs, show you how to read sentences and make them easier to understand. The comma is the most frequently-used form of punctuation.

My older brother brought pizza, popcorn, and soda to the party.

APOSTROPHE: The **apostrophe** indicates the place where letters have been removed in contractions (do not/don't). The apostrophe is also used to form the possessive of nouns (Bill's hat/the girls' team).

Whatever you do, don't sit on Jill's hat.

QUOTATION MARKS: **Quotation marks** indicate the exact words a person is saying. They enclose, or set off, a direct quotation. Quotation marks are also used to enclose the titles of short works such as short stories, short poems, paintings, songs, articles, speeches, chapters, and essays.

Bill shrugged and said, "If you want to go, take the car."

SEMICOLON: A **semicolon** is used in place of a coordinating conjunction to join two independent clauses and to emphasize the close relationship between the two. The semicolon is also used before such words as *accordingly, besides, consequently, hence, however, moreover, nevertheless, otherwise,* and *therefore.*

My mother plays the flute; my father plays the piano.
I was late for class; however, they hadn't begun the test yet.

COLON: A **colon** signals the importance of the information that follows it; it is used after the salutation in a business letter, before a list of specifics, and after the expressions *as follows* and *the following.* Colons are also used to separate; they are placed between the hour and minutes when writing the time (5:18 p.m.), and between the volume and number or volume and page number of a periodical (*Atlantic Monthly* 97:6 or *Newsworthy* 17:5-9).

Dear Sir:
Thank you for your recent letter.

A. *Directions:* Insert the correct punctuation where it is needed in the following sentences. You may add *'s* when necessary.
   EXAMPLE: "Why won't we read the story called 'The Lottery,' Ms. Knox?"

1. I dont really like Chips jacket said Hank
2. For the meal Mr. Perry cooked the following stuffed turkey mashed potatoes creamed onions and steamed green beans
3. I made the 150 p.m. mail pick-up with my letter to Poughkeepsie New York
4. No the article The Cold Facts about ice fishing is not in Sports Illustrated 34 9
5. When will your family be travelling to Italy Yugoslavia and Switzerland Earl
6. Help Ill never remember that President Kennedy was shot on November 22 1963
7. Jessies coach said sternly Just what do you think youre doing
8. Congress passed the Homestead Act in 1862 consequently people began to settle the plains of the West
9. I wont sing Shell Be Coming Around the Mountain with you
10. The batter hit the ball it landed high in the bleachers
11. Make sure you bring the following a flashlight sleeping bag canteen and tarpaulin
12. Come here Marina and do this word problem at the board said her mathematics teacher Miss Finnegan
13. Boil me in oil but I will never read The Autobiography of a Fast Food Fry Clerk
14. Ms. Tashigata brought her only dog Miss Misty Misfit to the dog show and won the blue ribbon in her class
15. Hasnt Henry finished Stephen Crane story The Open Boat
16. On December 7 1941 the Japanese bombed Pearl Harbor destroying much of the American naval fleet however the Americans rapidly replaced ships and went on to win the war
17. My mom goes to The Womens Health Club she likes to play racket ball there
18. When will you come over to Nancys house asked Jill

19. Why wont he learn that he cant just play basketball all the time hell never have time to do other activities

20. Your oldest brother Jim wanted to borrow my history book its on my desk

B. *Directions:* Circle any punctuation marks in the following letter that are used incorrectly. Add the punctuation needed to make the sentence correct.

1087 W. 57th Street
Boston. Massachusetts
January 22, 1994

The No Nonsense Stationery Company, Inc,
34 Grove Lane
Old Falls, Virginia

Dear Sir, or Madam:

Last March I placed an order for two gross of your no, 2 long envelopes and since then I have waited patiently to receive the envelopes. Every day I go to my mailbox as I walk I wonder to my dog; 'Where are they. Will they be in the box today. So far I've heard nothing from you. Did you receive my order? Im beginning to think you havent received it. If you had, you would have done the following; pull the box of envelopes, off the shelf, wrap them in brown paper, address them correctly and mail them! I havent received any package from you therefore I am writing to complain.

I am disappointed in your service! When I read about your company in *Mailing for Money* 9;1, I thought your company could supply what I wanted. Well! I was wrong. A reputable magazine like "Mailing for Money" shouldnt be accepting advertising from a shoddy company like your's. Its bad enough that I was misled but the magazine should protect others from making my mistake. All I have to say to you is "Take your envelopes and stuff them."

Sincerely.
I. M. N. Raged

5. FUNCTIONS OF PREPOSITIONAL PHRASES

The prepositional phrase always functions as either an adjective or an adverb. The adjective phrase, like an adjective, modifies a noun or pronoun. The adverb phrase modifies a verb, an adjective, or another adverb.

EXAMPLE: The cat (with the double paws) [ADJ] crept stealthily (through the garden) [ADV].

A. *Directions:* Put parentheses around each of the prepositional phrases in the following sentences. Then, depending on the function of that prepositional phrase, write **adjective** or **adverb** in the space provided at the end.
EXAMPLE: Juan hid (behind the curtain). _____adverb_____

1. Did you ask your teacher about the assignment?

   _____

2. Sandy finished her experiment before Don.

   _____

3. Her favorite ring went down the drain. _____

4. Everyone likes science fiction except Meagan.

   _____

5. The new girl is from Taiwan. _____

6. Like my mother, I gain weight very easily.

   _____

7. The library books about Francis Marion are missing.

   _____

8. Since the summer her playing has really improved.

   _____

9. The flowers were all facing toward the sun.

   _____

10. A litle pika scampered under that bush. _____

11. The people with cars are ready to go. _____

12. That dot high above the clouds must be a balloon.

_____

13. Kenyatta hid her diary beneath her mattress.

_____

14. Arthur went to the new park. _____

15. The Hungry Mind is the best bookstore in St. Paul.

_____

16. The heron flew across the lake. _____

17. She can't finish the game until tomorrow. _____

18. The argument between Beatrice and Joyce is silly.

_____

19. Robbie stirred the batter with a spoon. _____

20. How can you run around the track so fast?

_____

B. *Directions:* Put parentheses around the prepositional phrases in the following sentences. Then label them **ADJ** or **ADV**, depending on their function.

ADV
EXAMPLE: I slipped (on the ice).

THE RUSSIAN REVOLUTION

1. The Russian Revolution was one of the most influential events of the 20th century.

2. Actually there were two Russian Revolutions during 1917.

3. The first revolution, the February Revolution, was caused by a popular revolt.

4. The rioters were not famous revolutionaries but were ordinary people from St. Petersburg.

5. Cold, hunger, and despair drove them into the streets of the city.

6. The Russian ruler, Tsar Nicholas II, demanded help with the rioters from his soldiers.

7. To the tsar's dismay, the soldiers became an unreliable source of support.

8. Russia was fighting a war against Germany and sustaining an enormous number of casualties.

9. Soldiers were fighting far from home without guns or ammunition.

10. Few among them still supported the tsar's government.

11. The soldiers soon fought beside the people of St. Petersburg and against the tsar's few remaining supporters.

12. Rebellious railwaymen prevented Nicholas's return to St. Petersburg by train.

13. After a week of rioting, Nicholas II finally relinquished his rule.

14. Leaders established a new Provisional Government over Russia.

15. Between February and October this new government became unpopular with the Russian people.

16. The peasants wanted their own land and peace at any cost.

17. Amid this confusion Vladimir Ilyich Lenin returned from exile.

18. He and his small Bolshevik Party soon gained popularity with their slogan of "Peace, Land, and Bread."

19. By October the political situation approached anarchy.

20. In October the Bolsheviks overthrew the Provisional Government and established the world's first communist government.

C. *Directions:* Write one sentence for each of the prepositional phrases found below. Put parentheses around each prepositional phrase. Then label each phrase **ADJ** or **ADV** depending on its function.

EXAMPLE: in the water

> ADV
> I fell (in the water).

1. throughout the play

_____

2. across the table

_____

3. after class

_____

4. before the election

_____

5. with a turtle

_____

6. into the crowd

_____

7. in a rage

_____

8. under a heavy rock

_____

9. until vacation

_____

10. inside the cage

_____

11. from severe allergies

_____

12. among the poisonous snakes

_____

13. at midnight

_____

14. behind the bushes

_____

15. like my teacher

_____

16. around the forest

_____

17. beneath the earth's surface

_____

18. in the tea leaves

_____

19. to the party

_____

20. out the window

_____

6. ERRORS

A. *Directions:* Each of the following sentences contains at least one error. Rewrite each sentence correctly in the space provided.

EXAMPLE: Myra cried, "Dont you take the last piece of cake"!
Myra cried, "Don't you take the last piece of cake!"

1. Like her cousin Chris read "Light in the Forest" over vacation.

   _____

2. Before you go to school, will you walk Amoses dog.

   _____

3. Its quite clear to me that *Alice in Wonderland* is more than just a fairy tale.

   _____

4. Help, I dont remember the address.

   _____

5. Adam babysat last night at the Anderson's house, the baby stayed up past their bedtime.

   _____

6. One of the students were chosen for the part.

   _____

7. Enid gave her uncle Ed several albums for his birthday?

   _____

8. Maybelle said, "your the only one who did'nt come."

   _____

9. Either James or Fred are giving his oral report!

   _____

10. "Will you be going to the Grand Canyon this summer" asked Gillian?

    _____

11. Carlos bright, red balloon tugged at his wrist.

    _____

12. Please do as follows; underline each noun and label it's function.

    _____

13. On july 16; 1974 Senna won the marathon.

_____

14. Darnelle carefully moved the slide into place, then he focused the microscope.

_____

_____

15. Both her brothers and Lucy seems happy at the childrens party.

_____

16. Jessica asked whether the notebook was your's?

_____

17. Elizabeth was late to school for her alarm clock had not rung.

_____

18. "My Old Kentucky Home" is the anthem of the Kentucky derby.

_____

19. My brother felt badly after his flu shot.

_____

20. The oxen on Ms. Millers farm is considered the best in the county.

_____

B. *Directions:* Each of the following sentences contains at least one error. Rewrite each sentence correctly in the space provided.
   EXAMPLE: At the next meeting of the rotary club, uncle Joe will gives a speech.
   At the next meeting of the Rotary Club, Uncle Joe will give a speech.

1. Daffy duck and Porky pig is a popular cartoon character.

_____

2. My Father thinks its the last day for going to the carnival.

_____

3. You must begin the letter "Dear Sir or madam:" and end it with a closing and you're signature.

_____

_____

4. every summer we go to visit my grandparents in florence Italy.

_____

5. My mother brought home from the supermarket these items; ham, pinto beans; milk, eggs, cereal and vanilla flavoring.

   _____

   _____

6. Make sure your careful when you go camping for example put out all fires when leaving camp, boil all drinking water, and look out for bears.

   _____

   _____

7. At the beginning of the play, either Mary ellen or Althea and Cora Jean comes out on stage and sing a song.

   _____

   _____

8. Why dont you send Jimmy a post card from lake Erie.

   _____

9. Sally gave her only goldfish Jasper two much food and now she has no goldfish.

   _____

   _____

10. Myth says that the Hundred-handed Children went below the earth to make volcanoes such as mt. Etna in Sicily erupts.

    _____

    _____

11. At the beginning of class, Mr. Achebe asked, "how many of you has completed the assignment?".

    _____

    _____

12. Neither my aunt nor my grandmother are traveling by the Santa Fe railroad to her new house in the West.

    _____

    _____

13. Under president Jefferson the United State's of America doubled it's size with the Louisiana purchase.

    _____

    _____

14. Many people think *America The Beautiful* should be the national anthem because its easier to sing than our present anthem.

   _____

   _____

15. Lets read "The New Yorker" 32;6 for our report.

   _____

16. Kushina and her brother finished their chores, then they go to the movies

   _____

   _____

17. My mother wonders about "where all the shampoo goes?"

   _____

18. Mr. O'Shaughnessy always borrows the Marxes lawn mower, but never return it.

   _____

   _____

19. I did'nt do my homework on time, consequently I can't go to the little League all-stars game.

   _____

   _____

20. without a doubt my dog is the stupidest one in the entire town of Wheeling west Virginia.

   _____

   _____

PART II.
NEW MATERIAL

7. INTRODUCTION TO DEPENDENT CLAUSES

Read the following groups of words. Then underline the subjects once and the verbs twice.

1. that I saw in Switzerland
2. when she gets home from work
3. whom Roger met in class

Are these groups of words sentences? If you answered "yes," read them again. Although the above groups of words, like sentences, contain subjects and verbs, they do not express complete thoughts. In their present form they are only sentence fragments.

> **Definition**
> A **clause** is any group of words that contains a subject and verb. If a clause contains a subject and verb *and* expresses a complete thought, it is a simple sentence, or independent clause. A **dependent clause**, on the other hand, contains a subject and verb but does *not* express a complete thought and cannot stand alone. In other words, a dependent clause can be part of a sentence, but it cannot be a sentence in its own right. Dependent clauses are sometimes called **subordinate clauses**.

Look again at the three dependent clauses above. The words *that*, *whom*, and *when* are the introductory words in these clauses. Other examples of introductory words are *what*, *which*, *since*, *whose*, *after*, *where*, and *although*. Introductory words join a dependent clause to an independent clause.

Read the following sentences:

1. I loved the scenery *that I saw in Switzerland*.
2. My mom always exercises *when she gets home from work*.
3. Jane Dixon is the girl *whom Roger met in class*.

The dependent clauses above have been combined with independent clauses to form sentences. In each case the dependent clause adds some new piece of information to the sentence. Whereas the dependent clauses cannot stand by themselves as sentences, however, the independent, or **main clauses**, can:

1. I loved the scenery.
2. My mom always exercises.
3. Jane Dixon is the girl.

When an independent clause stands alone, it is called a simple sentence. It is called an independent clause only when it is combined with one or more dependent clauses into a sentence.

FUNCTIONS OF DEPENDENT CLAUSES

You have already learned that prepositional phrases can function as either adjectives or adverbs. Like phrases, dependent clauses function as grammatical units in a sentence. Depending on how they are used, dependent clauses can function as adjectives, adverbs, or nouns.

8. ADJECTIVE CLAUSES

Read the following sentences and answer the questions in the spaces provided:

1. The man *who owned the rocket* disappeared.

   Which man? _____

2. I saw the movie *that my sister recommended*.

   Which movie? _____

3. Al's grandmother grew up at a time *when there was no television*.

   Which time? _____

In each of these sentences, the italicized words give you more information about a noun in the sentence. For example, in sentence 1 you know that you are reading about a particular man—the man *who owned the rocket*. In sentence 2 you are not hearing about any old movie, but one that the speaker's sister recommended. And in sentence 3 you are reading about a specific time in history, a time before the invention of television. Without the italicized words, then, you know much less about the nouns *man*, *movie*, and *time*.

> **Definition**
> The italicized words in the above sentences are all examples of adjective clauses. An **adjective clause** is a dependent clause that functions as an adjective. Like all clauses, adjective clauses contain subjects and verbs. Like adjectives, they modify nouns and pronouns.

Most adjective clauses begin with one of the five relative pronouns: *who, whom, whose, which,* or *that*. A **relative pronoun** is a pronoun that introduces an adjective clause and refers or *relates* to another word in the sentence. In sentence 1 above, the relative pronoun *who* refers to the noun *man*. The word to which a relative pronoun refers—in this case, *man*—is called the **antecedent** of the pronoun—it *goes before* the pronoun.

Adjective clauses may also be introduced by the adverbs *when* and *where*:

1. That was an era *when everyone was poor*.
2. We moved to a state *where the sheep outnumbered the people*.

Adverbs that introduce adjective clauses are called **relative adverbs**.

Sometimes the relative pronouns *that* or *whom* may be omitted from an adjective clause altogether. In these cases the relative pronoun is *understood*, even though it is missing from the sentence:

1. The college (that) *Laura attended* is located in Idaho.
2. The teacher (whom) *John liked* moved.

In sentence 1 the relative pronoun *that* is understood; in sentence 2 the relative pronoun *whom* has been omitted.

THE FUNCTIONS OF RELATIVE PRONOUNS

The relative pronoun can sometimes serve as the subject of an adjective clause:

1. The ship, *which is enormous*, leaves in the morning.
2. The police caught the man *who robbed the bank*.

In sentence 1 the relative pronoun *which* is the subject of the verb *is*. The relative pronoun *who* is the subject of the verb *robbed* in sentence 2.

Relative pronouns can also function as direct objects, possessives, and objects of the preposition in adjective clauses:

1. The boy *whom I saw yesterday* has red hair. (*Whom* is a direct object.)
2. Mr. Tartabell, *whose wife is a lawyer*, knows Tina's father. (*Whose* is a possessive.)
3. The book *in which Ron saw the picture* came from the library. (*Which* is the object of the preposition *in*.)

Notice the use of the relative pronoun *whom* in sentence 1. In general, use *who* if the relative pronoun is the subject of a dependent clause and *whom* if the relative pronoun is not the subject. Also notice that when a relative pronoun is the object of a preposition, the preposition counts as the first word of the adjective clause.

ESSENTIAL AND NONESSENTIAL CLAUSES

Adjective clauses are either essential or nonessential to the sentences in which they appear. An **essential clause**, as its name suggests, is necessary to the meaning of a sentence. Essential clauses identify a particular person or thing, so leaving them out changes the meaning of a sentence or turns it into a nonsense sentence. **Nonessential clauses**, on the other hand, add information about the words they modify but are not essential to the meaning of a sentence:

1. "The Necklace" is the only story *that I really loved*. (This sentence does not make sense without the italicized clause. In this case the adjective clause is essential to the meaning of the sentence.)

2. "The Necklace," *which was first published in the nineteenth century*, is my favorite story. (Leaving out the italicized clause does not change the basic meaning of the sentence. In this case the adjective clause adds information, but is not essential.)

If you are not sure whether an adjective clause is essential or nonessential, try reading the sentence without the clause. If the clause is nonessential, the basic meaning of the sentence will not change; however, omitting an essential clause *will* change the meaning of the sentence. For example, first read the following sentence with the adjective clause, and then read it again without the clause:

Doctors, *who spend years in school*, usually earn high salaries.

Although the adjective clause adds information to the sentence, removing it does not change the basic meaning of the sentence. Now try the test again on another sentence:

Doctors *who fail their medical examinations* should not practice medicine.

Removing the adjective clause destroys the meaning of this sentence. Here the adjective clause is essential.

PUNCTUATION

A nonessential adjective clause is set off from the rest of a sentence by commas. If the clause comes at the end of a sentence, use one comma before it. If the clause appears in the middle of a sentence, use a comma on either side of it. Do not use any commas with essential clauses:

1. I work for Mr. Jenkins, who moved here from Nevada in 1976. (nonessential)
2. Mt. Everest, which is part of the Himalayas, is a dangerous mountain. (nonessential)
3. There goes the dog that I saw yesterday! (essential)

HINTS

a. Adjective clauses usually appear right after the nouns or pronouns they modify.

> The monster *that ate Chicago* is green. (*That ate Chicago* modifies the noun *monster*.)

> Jan has a brother who flies kites. (*Who flies kites* modifies the noun *brother*.)

b. Adjective clauses modify words *outside* the clause. They never modify words inside the clause.

c. Be careful how you use the relative pronouns *that* and *which* with essential and nonessential adjective clauses. Although you may use either *that* or *which* with essential clauses, *that* is preferred in most cases. With nonessential clauses, on the other hand, use only *which*.

ADJECTIVE CLAUSE EXERCISES

A. *Directions:* Enclose each adjective clause in parentheses. Then write the word the clause modifies in the space provided at the end of each sentence.

EXAMPLE: I like the cat (that sits in the window).

_____cat_____

1. The mansion, which sits on the top of a large hill, looks ancient.

   _____

2. The man who ate dinner here last night was Prince Charles.

   _____

3. Bernice wore the dress that she bought in Greece.

   _____

4. Virginia Woolf, whose father was a Victorian writer, wrote modern novels.   _____

5. The man whom we met on the bus collects rocks.

   _____

6. Archeological research revealed the exact spot where the tomb was located.   _____

7. The nineteenth century was a time when women were often treated as inferiors.   _____

8. Las Vegas is a city to which gamblers flock by the thousands.

   _____

9. The record you bought yesterday is horrible.

   _____

10. Richard Wright, whose most famous novel is *Native Son*, died in 1960.   _____

11. Kilchurn Castle, which is located in Scotland, is a lovely building.

    _____

12. Renee likes stories that frighten her.   _____

13. Ms. Minifie remembers the days when farmers used horses to plow the fields.   _____

14. The rock star Jacques loves has purple hair.

_____

15. The box in which I found the hammer fell overboard.

_____

16. In Beijing, which is the capital of China, many people ride bicycles. _____

17. The puppy that is barking in the window is for sale.

_____

18. The store where Joni bought the glasses went bankrupt.

_____

19. The man to whom I owe my life won a medal.

_____

20. Marty lost the grammar book I gave him. _____

B. *Directions:* Enclose each adjective clause in parentheses. Then write the word the clause modifies in the space provided at the end of each sentence.
EXAMPLE: The team (that I support) lost. _____team_____

WOODY GUTHRIE: DUSTBOWL BALLADEER

1. Woody Guthrie, who was an important American folksinger, was born in 1912. _____

2. Woody, whose parents named him after President Woodrow Wilson, grew up in Oklahoma. _____

3. The town in which Woody lived, Okemah, was a small farming town. _____

4. The period when Woody grew up was a difficult time for farmers.

_____

5. Many of the people whom Woody knew were poor.

_____

6. The jobs that Woody's father held never lasted long.

_____

7. Clara, who was Woody's sister, died in a fire.

_____

8. Woody's mother died from a hereditary illness that is called Huntington's Disease. _____

9. The Great Depression, which started in 1929, was hard on Oklahoma. _____

10. A drought turned soil that had once been rich into dust.

_____

11. This was the era when dust storms filled the air.

_____

12. During this period Woody bought a guitar, which he soon learned to play. _____

13. Woody began to write and sing songs about the people who were losing their farms and moving to California.

_____

14. He played these songs, which came to be known as the *Dust Bowl Ballads*, all over the country. _____

15. Woody, whose fame soon began to grow, wrote hundreds of songs during the next two decades. _____

16. Many of the songs that he wrote became folk classics.

_____

17. "This Land Is Your Land," which Woody wrote as a young man, is now known to almost every American. _____

18. Folksinger Bob Dylan, who was strongly influenced by Woody's music, met Woody in 1961. _____

19. By then the disease that killed his mother had already kept Woody in the hospital for eight years. _____

20. Woody's son, whose name is Arlo, has continued to sing and record his father's songs since Woody's death in 1967.

_____

C. *Directions:* Enclose each adjective clause in parentheses and underline the relative pronoun. Then write the function of the relative pronoun in the space provided.

EXAMPLE: Jeb, (<u>who</u> is my brother), hates snakes.
_____subject_____

1. Winston Churchill, whom I greatly admire, was a powerful speaker.

   _____

2. The Nineteenth Amendment, which was ratified in 1920, gave women the right to vote. _____

3. The woman whose wallet I found gave me a reward.

   _____

4. Mr. Fisher, to whom I owe my success, was a great and gifted teacher. _____

5. The car that I usually drive broke down yesterday.

   _____

6. Alfred Hitchcock, who directed many great movies, grew up in England. _____

7. *The New Yorker*, for which many famous writers have worked, is a respected magazine. _____

8. Eleanor Roosevelt, whose work for the less fortunate won her many admirers, died in 1963. _____

9. The man who fishes with my grandfather has red hair.

   _____

10. The radio that I found at the dump works.

    _____

D. *Directions:* Enclose each adjective clause in parentheses. Then indicate whether it is an essential or nonessential clause in the space provided at the end of the sentence.

EXAMPLE: Mr. Dill, (who lost a leg in the war), is very active.
<u>nonessential</u>

1. The fish that I bought today is not fresh. _____

2. Steve, who sits next to me in math class, is very funny.

   _____

3. That is the neighborhood where the gang meets.

   _____

4. I once visited the San Diego Zoo, which is one of the best zoos in the United States. _____

5. My brother who lives in China is my favorite brother.
_____

6. Mr. Wilson, whose dog once bit my cat, has a bad temper.
_____

7. The fourteenth century was a period when many people died of the plague. _____

8. The city of Buffalo, where many people eat chicken wings, has severe winters. _____

9. The musicians I wanted to meet left this morning.
_____

10. I recently read *The Crucible*, which is a play about the Salem witch trials. _____

11. Mr. Mitchell, to whom Jeb sold his car, likes fried squid.
_____

12. I never saw the herons that lived in the swamp behind my house.
_____

E. *Directions:* Rewrite each pair of sentences as one sentence with an adjective clause. Then enclose each adjective clause in parentheses. Be sure to punctuate your sentences correctly.

EXAMPLE: Mr. Rover is a friendly man. He is my dentist.
    Mr. Rover, (who is my dentist), is a friendly man.

1. Abraham Lincoln was our sixteenth president. He was assassinated in 1865.
_____

2. Mr. Tortellini knows my father. His son is my best friend.
_____

3. Bertram read a book. It belongs to the library.
_____

4. That enormous rhinoceros is dangerous. It lives in our basement.
_____

5. The politician lost. Randy supported her in the election.
_____

6. That is the city. My car was stolen there.

   _____

7. The elf is real. I saw it through my window.

   _____

8. Maxine remembers the old days. Life was simpler then.

   _____

9. The game of basketball has changed over the years. Basketball was invented in Massachusetts.

   _____

10. The doctor studied medicine in Europe. We know his children.

   _____

11. My favorite literary character is Dr. Watson. He was a close friend of Sherlock Holmes.

   _____

12. The blizzard buried her car. It struck without warning.

   _____

13. Ms. Feldberg loves politics. She has a one-track mind.

   _____

14. Springfield is the town. John and Gillian grew up there.

   _____

15. The man is grateful. Joan sacrificed her life for him.

   _____

16. The Battle of Britain was a crucial battle in World War II. It took place in the summer of 1940.

   _____

17. The car ran over our television. It was a convertible.

   _____

18. Dorrie's cat eats mice. Its name is Alice.

   _____

19. Genghis Kahn was a Mongol conqueror. He died in 1227.

   _____

20. The bird is an owl. Sabrina saw it on her roof.

   _____

F. *Directions:* Using the relative pronouns or adverbs listed below, write ten sentences of your own that contain adjective clauses. Then enclose each adjective clause in parentheses. Be sure to punctuate your sentences correctly.

EXAMPLE: who   Ms. Pakula, (who knows my mother), lives next door.

1. which

_____

2. whom

_____

3. that

_____

4. when

_____

5. who

_____

6. whose

_____

7. which

_____

8. where

_____

9. whom

_____

10. that

_____

9. ADVERB CLAUSES

Read the following sentences. Then answer the questions in the spaces provided:

1. *When she saw her sister's face,* Sonia hid in the closet.
   What is the independent clause here? _____
   When did Sonia hide? _____
2. *Wherever he leads them,* Sidney's friends will follow.
   What is the independent clause here? _____
   Where will Sidney's friends follow? _____
3. The lion growled *as though it wanted to escape.*
   What is the independent clause here? _____
   How did the lion growl? _____
4. Roy's aunt will call him *if she remembers his birthday.*
   What is the independent clause here? _____
   Under what conditions will Roy's aunt call him? _____

As you probably realized, the non-italicized words are the independent clauses in each of the above sentences. You may also have noticed that the italicized words—the dependent clauses—answer the second question after each sentence. For example, the answer to the question *When did Sonia hide?* is *When she saw her sister's face.* In each of these sentences, the dependent clauses give you more information about the independent clauses. In particular, the dependent clauses tell you something about the verbs in the independent clauses. They tell you *when* Sonia *hid, where* Sidney's friends *will follow, how* the lion *growled,* and *under what conditions* Roy's aunt *will call.*

> **Definition**
> The italicized words in the above sentences are all examples of adverb clauses. An **adverb clause** is a dependent clause that functions as an adverb. Like adverbs, adverb clauses usually modify verbs. They tell *how, when, where, why,* and *under what conditions* the action of a verb is completed.

1. Whenever Maria visits, my father bakes bread. (The adverb clause *whenever Maria visits* modifies the verb *bakes.*)
2. Lonny saw where the toad went. (The adverb clause *where the toad went* modifies the verb *saw.*)

Adverb clauses sometimes modify adjectives and adverbs too:

3. Amahl was certain *that he could walk.* (The adverb clause *that he could walk* modifies the adjective *certain.*)
4. Catarina understands computers better *than Chuck does.* (The adverb clause *than Chuck does* modifies the adverb *better.*)

The words that introduce adverb clauses are called **subordinate conjunctions**. These words join the adverb clause to the rest of the sentence. Some of the most common subordinate conjunctions are grouped below according to the questions they answer:

> *How?* although, as, as if, as though, than
> *When?* after, as, as long as, as soon as, before, since, until, when, whenever, while
> *Where?* where, wherever, whence, whither
> *Why?* as, because, in order that, since, so that, that
> *Under what conditions?* although, as long as, even though, if, provided that, though, unless, whereas, whether, while

Subordinate conjunctions can have more than one meaning. Consequently, some of them are included in several of the categories above.

INCOMPLETE ADVERB CLAUSES

Adverb clauses from which words have been omitted are said to be **elliptical**, or incomplete. In the same way that the relative pronouns omitted from adjective clauses are understood, the words missing from incomplete adverb clauses are understood in the reader's mind:

1. Charles Dickens wrote more novels *than Jane Austen* [did].
2. *When* [he was] *painting*, Cezanne hated to be interrupted.

In the above sentences the words *did* and *he was* may be omitted from the adverb clauses. The resulting clauses are elliptical but correct.

PUNCTUATION

Insert a comma after an introductory adverb clause:

1. *After I saw the game,* I took a taxi to the airport.
2. *Unless he changes his mind,* Tom isn't going to camp.

In general, do *not* use a comma before an adverb clause that ends a sentence. Insert a comma before a concluding adverb clause only when you are using the subordinate conjunctions *for, although,* and *though,* or when you are using *as* and *since* to mean *because:*

1. I do not know *when Jan won the medal.*
2. Seymour waited patiently *until Uma returned from the store.*

3. Jane did not win the election, *although she had worked very hard to become class president*.

HINT Adverb clauses usually appear at the beginning or end of a sentence. Adjective clauses, on the other hand, appear in the middle or at the end of a sentence, but *not* at the beginning.

ADVERB CLAUSE EXERCISES

A. *Directions:* Enclose each adverb clause in parentheses. Then write the word the clause modifies in the space provided at the end of each sentence.

EXAMPLE: (Before the storm began), Hal shut the windows.

_____ shut _____

1. Since Susannah had no work to do, she read another chapter in her book.

_____

2. As he read his speech, Paul's confidence grew.

_____

3. You will miss your train unless you leave immediately.

_____

4. Rosetta is older than her sister. _____

5. Erving watched her thoughtfully as she walked across the room.

_____

6. When we were seniors in high school, we ate doughnuts every day. _____

7. The explorer went where no person had ever set foot before.

_____

8. I will continue to drink diet soda until the sun goes down.

_____

9. While swimming, Charlotte heard someone call to her.

_____

10. Although he died young, John Keats led a full life.

_____

11. Work hard so that you can go home early. _____

12. We missed the spelling bee since we did not pick up our tickets on time. _____

13. After she had spent two weeks in the woods, Doris realized she hated camping. _____

14. Because Moby Dick bit off his leg, Captain Ahab vowed to kill the great white whale. _____

15. Karen looks as innocent as a baby. _____

16. I see them play whenever they come to town.

    _____

17. They talked about old times while the dinner burned in the oven.

    _____

18. When writing a speech, the governor is usually grumpy.

    _____

19. My dog is bigger than your dog. _____

20. I liked the play at first, though I changed my mind later.

    _____

B. *Directions:* Enclose each adverb clause in parentheses. Then write the word the clause modifies in the space provided at the end of each sentence.
   EXAMPLE: Dale answered (when Roy called). ____answered____

FROM TSAR TO REVOLUTION

1. The tsars ruled Russia until the Russian Revolution occurred in 1917. _____

2. Tsars were like kings, though they possessed even greater powers.

   _____

3. Ivan the Great unified Russia when he defeated the Mongols in the fifteenth century. _____

4. After he expanded Russia's territory, Ivan the Terrible took the title "tsar of all Russia" in 1547. _____

5. Ivan the Terrible was much crueler than Ivan the Great.

   _____

6. When Tsar Boris Godunov died in 1605, Russia experienced the "Time of Troubles." _____

7. This period lasted until the Poles invaded and were expelled in 1612 and 1613. _____

8. Because Michael Romanov became tsar in 1613, a new dynasty began that year. _____

9. When Peter the Great became tsar in 1682, he tried to make Russia more like western Europe. _____

10. Peter enacted many reforms so that Russia would be westernized.
_____

11. After Peter founded St. Petersburg in 1703, the new city became the capital of Russia. _____

12. Although Catherine the Great was not the first female tsar, she was the most powerful of these tsars. _____

13. Whereas Catherine expanded Russia's borders, she also expanded the institution of serfdom. _____

14. The wealthy landowners restricted the rights of the serfs so that these peasants would become like slaves. _____

15. If you were a serf, you had no freedom. _____

16. Since the tsars were harsh rulers, many revolutionary groups tried to overthrow them in the nineteenth century.
_____

17. These revolutionaries feared for Russia's future unless the country had a new form of government. _____

18. After they assassinated Alexander II in 1881, many of these revolutionaries were executed. _____

19. When a spontaneous revolution swept Tsar Nicholas I from power in early 1917, a liberal government was formed.
_____

20. This liberal government ruled until Vladimir Lenin and the Bolsheviks overthrew it in October of 1917. _____

C. *Directions:* Rewrite each of the following sentences by moving the adverb clause. Be sure to punctuate your new sentences correctly.

EXAMPLE: I will get on the horse when I am ready.

When I am ready, I will get on the horse.

1. Unless you change your mind, Romaine won't go.

_____

2. Since I started it, I haven't been able to put the book down.

_____

3. President Richard Nixon resigned after a damaging tape was revealed.

_____

4. Doris has to go outside and shovel whenever it snows.

_____

5. Before he wrote the book about cockroaches, Christopher Bym was a journalist.

_____

6. Bart has no desire to see Hawaii, though he has never been there.

_____

7. While I was doing my laundry, my cat ate the chicken.

_____

8. Because he did not approve of their behavior, Martin left the room.

_____

9. I will be rich as soon as I become famous.

_____

10. The United States stayed out of World War II until Pearl Harbor was attacked.

_____

11. Dr. Marquez will go wherever he is needed.

_____

12. You may see the movie provided that you take your sister.

_____

D. *Directions:* Rewrite each pair of sentences as one sentence with an adverb clause. Then enclose each adverb clause in parentheses. Be sure to punctuate your sentences correctly.

EXAMPLE: I saw Jim. Then I saw Shawn.
(After I saw Jim), I saw Shawn.

1. Cuthbert loves the ocean. Cuthbert never learned to swim.

   _____

2. I will not leave. I refuse to miss my dinner.

   _____

3. The dance ended. Cinderella went home in her coach.

   _____

4. We moved to Tennessee. No one calls us any more.

   _____

5. Jeanette and Phil were watching a movie. It started to rain.

   _____

6. Paulette looked beautiful. She looked like an angel.

   _____

7. Terrence saw a spider. He fainted.

   _____

8. Renada plays in the rain. She always gets sick the next day.

   _____

9. Ms. Pronto's class planned a picnic. Later they heard it would snow.

   _____

10. Stuart might not finish his homework. He may not be able to see the movie with us.

   _____

11. The atom bomb is a deadly weapon. The hydrogen bomb is even more destructive.

   _____

12. Chico went to the mall. Rosalita joined him there later.

   _____

13. Basil saw a movie about zombies. He hasn't slept for a week.

   _____

14. The city of Rome burned. The emperor Nero just played the fiddle.

   _____

15. Thurmon saw his little brother. He ducked into an alley.

   _____

E. *Directions:* Enclose each dependent clause in parentheses. Then indicate in the space provided at the end of each sentence whether the clause is an *adjective* or *adverb* clause.
   EXAMPLE: The car (that lost its wheel) stopped quickly.
   _____adjective_____

1. Since I ate the eels, I have felt sick. _____

2. The train whose whistle you hear just left. _____

3. Napoleon lost most of his army after he invaded Russia.

   _____

4. Because he asked for more gruel, Oliver Twist was severely punished. _____

5. Madrid, which is the capital of Spain, is a beautiful city.

   _____

6. Nora will go wherever her employer sends her.

   _____

7. The rats that I saw at the dump scurried away quickly.

   _____

8. Although she has never eaten chocolate ants, Betsy is willing to try anything. _____

9. Our new house is bigger than our old apartment.

   _____

10. The town in which I was born disappeared last Friday.

    _____

11. As soon as we get back from dinner, let's play cards.

    _____

12. Eugene O'Neill, whom some feel is America's greatest playwright, was not a happy man. _____

13. Philadelphia is the city where the U.S. Constitution was written.

    _____

14. The sheriff won't rest until he catches the horse thief.

_____

15. While I was touring the factory, a fire broke out.

_____

16. Those were the days when you didn't have to lock your house at night. _____

17. While fishing, Petula was eaten by a shark. _____

18. Robert Louis Stevenson, who was born in Scotland, died in Samoa.

_____

19. Akeem hurried to the theater so that he would be first in line.

_____

20. Keela is the girl whose mother won a Nobel Prize.

_____

F. *Directions:* Using the subordinate conjunctions indicated below, write ten sentences of your own that contain adverb clauses. Then enclose each adverb clause in parentheses. Be sure to punctuate your sentences correctly.

EXAMPLE: when   (When Sue left), she forgot her dog.

1. if

_____

2. although

_____

3. since

_____

4. unless

_____

5. before

_____

6. because

_____

7. until

_____

8. than

_____

9. where

_____

10. as

_____

10. NOUN CLAUSES

You have already learned to identify adjective and adverb clauses. Now see if you can identify the dependent clauses in the following sentences. Then answer the questions in the spaces provided:

1. *What I believe* is none of your business.

   What is the main verb? _____

   What is the subject of this sentence? _____

2. Stella knew *why she lost the lead role*.

   What is the main verb? _____

   What is the direct object in this sentence? _____

3. Doreen's answer was *what Chick wanted to hear*.

   What is the main verb? _____

   What is the predicate noun in this sentence? _____

If you said that the italicized words in the above sentences are the dependent clauses, give yourself a gold star. If, on the other hand, you had trouble answering the second question after each sentence, don't worry. They were tricky questions. In the above sentences the dependent clauses function as the subject in one case, the direct object in another, and the predicate noun in the third. In other words, *What I believe* is the subject of sentence 1, *why she lost the lead role* is the direct object in sentence 2, and *what Chick wanted to hear* is the predicate noun in sentence 3. The main verbs of these three sentences are *is*, *knew*, and *was*.

Definition
The italicized words in the above sentences are all examples of noun clauses. A **noun clause** is a dependent clause that functions as a noun. Like nouns, noun clauses have specific functions in sentences: they can function as subjects, direct objects, indirect objects, objects of the preposition, and predicate nouns.

---

1. *How that man juggles with his eyes shut* astounds me. (subject)
2. Do you know *whether the tornado is coming this way*? (direct object)
3. The millionaire gave *whoever liked him* a thousand dollars. (indirect object)

4. The moral of the story is *that turkeys shouldn't celebrate Thanksgiving.* (predicate noun)
5. The pioneers survived the winter with *whatever fuel they could find.* (object of the preposition)

Notice that in sentence 5 the preposition *with* is not part of the noun clause. That's because the entire noun clause is the object of the preposition. Be careful not to confuse this kind of clause with adjective clauses that *do* sometimes begin with prepositions:

The house *in which Jules lives* is haunted.

If you have trouble telling the difference between an adjective clause and a noun clause that is functioning as an object of the preposition, ask yourself this question: "Does the clause modify, or tell me something about, the noun that precedes it?" If it does, the clause is probably an adjective clause. In the above sentence, for instance, the adjective clause *in which Jules lives* tells you which house you are reading about. On the other hand, the clause *whatever fuel they could find* does not modify the noun *winter* in sentence 5.

Noun clauses begin either with relative pronouns like *who*, *that*, or *which* or with subordinate conjunctions like *why*, *how*, or *if*. Compounds like *whoever* and *whatever* are also used to introduce noun clauses. Below is a list of the words that frequently introduce noun clauses:

if	when	whoever
how	where	whom
that	which	whomever
what	whichever	whose
whatever	who	whosoever

OMITTING THE INTRODUCTORY WORD

When people speak or write sentences with noun clauses, they sometimes leave out the relative pronoun or subordinate conjunction that introduces the clause. For example, the introductory word *that* is often left out:

1. I know [that] *you are watching me.*
2. Raphael believes [that] *his sister is a Martian.*

The introductory word in a noun clause is usually omitted in direct quotations, too:

3. Ben said, *"I have always wanted to see a penguin."*
4. *"May I have a cookie?"* the president asked.

Apart from not having introductory words, noun clauses that are direct quotations always function as direct objects. In sentences 3 and 4, for example, the noun clauses answer the direct object questions *What did Ben say?* and *What did the president ask?*

There are no special rules of punctuation for noun clauses. Generally, however, noun clauses are not set off with commas.

HINT When you remove adjective and adverb clauses from sentences, the words that are left usually form a complete sentence. Sentences containing noun clauses are different. With the noun clause removed, they are no longer complete sentences in most cases:

1. *Why Sandy plays the flute* is not clear.
2. The answer is *whatever you want it to be*.

NOUN CLAUSE EXERCISES

A. *Directions:* Enclose each noun clause in parentheses. Then write the function of the clause in the space provided at the end of each sentence.

EXAMPLE: She demanded (that the police release her).
    <u> direct object </u>

1. What the dictator said made me tremble. _____

2. The theme of the lecture was that bees like honey.

   _____

3. I discovered who took the pies. _____

4. Mr. Bishop will give the reward money to whatever charity you choose. _____

5. My sister drew whomever she saw a picture.

   _____

6. Matu asked, "Why do we always have fish sticks for breakfast?"

   _____

7. That you are even here is a tribute to your courage.

   _____

8. A new job is what you need. _____

9. The government offered whoever didn't pay taxes a second chance.

   _____

10. When you buy your tickets makes all the difference.

    _____

11. Rick realized he had never seen her before. _____

12. Juan will travel with whoever is taking the tour.

    _____

13. Have you ever wondered if other people live in the universe?

    _____

14. Hansel and Gretel's main concern was how they would find their
    way home. _____

15. Whatever route you choose will take a long time.

    _____

16. The judge will give whatever you say her careful consideration.

    _____

17. "Now I understand," Joe said with a smile.

    _____

18. Where Jim and Robin will get married hasn't been decided yet.

    _____

19. I promise to be back at whatever time you like.

    _____

20. Romeo could tell she didn't love him any more.

    _____

B. *Directions:* Enclose each noun clause in parentheses. Then write the
   function of the clause in the space provided at the end of the sentence.
   EXAMPLE: The blue dress is (what she wanted). <u>predicate noun</u>

   1. Why Emily Dickinson avoided most people is not clear.

      _____

   2. A career in journalism is what Horace once wanted.

      _____

   3. Did you know that Katherine Anne Porter died at the age of 91?

      _____

   4. Mort will bake whomever he wishes a pie. _____

   5. I will build the boat with whatever tools are available.

      _____

   6. Some people still wonder if the world is flat.

      _____

   7. Why you got that suntan puzzles me. _____

8. The question now is how you solved the mystery.

   _____

9. The station will give free concert tickets to whoever requests them.

   _____

10. I will give whichever you choose my stamp of approval.

    _____

11. The investigation will reveal whose mistake caused the crash.

    _____

12. When I will see you again is not entirely clear.

    _____

13. Jesse will tutor you in math at whatever time is best.

    _____

14. "I've never seen a mountain," Bert said sadly.

    _____

15. The college provides whoever needs it a scholarship.

    _____

16. Lana's excuse was that her little brother ate her homework.

    _____

17. That I even made the semi-finals amazed me.

    _____

18. Can you tell which toothpaste works better?

    _____

19. Mr. Mandell gave money to whichever candidate his wife chose.

    _____

20. Zeus thundered, "Your days are numbered, mortal."

    _____

C. *Directions:* Complete the following sentences by filling in the blanks with noun clauses.
   EXAMPLE: <u>What this poem means</u> is anybody's guess.

   1. The real problem is _____.
   2. Grandma insisted _____.
   3. _____ seemed ridiculous.
   4. The disc jockey gave _____ a free ticket.
   5. I will show the photographs to _____.

6. Many people have questioned _____.

7. The moral of the fable is _____.

8. _____ contradicts what you said before.

9. Seymour made the rocket with _____.

10. The camp counselor told _____ terrifying ghost stories.

D. *Directions:* Enclose each dependent clause in parentheses. Then indicate the function of each clause in the space provided at the end of the sentence.

S for subject	OP for object of the preposition
DO for direct object	ADJ for adjective
IO for indirect object	ADV for adverb
PN for predicate noun	

EXAMPLE: I see (what you are doing)! _____DO_____

1. How Britain lost its empire is not clear to me.

   _____

2. Although I have no money, I am still happy.

   _____

3. Rabies, which is often transmitted by animals, is a horrible illness.

   _____

4. The real mystery is why Stan ever wanted a pet buzzard.

   _____

5. The town where we are going has no movie theaters.

   _____

6. Bryan did not know what he wanted for his birthday.

   _____

7. Francie saw the Sphinx after she climbed the Great Pyramid.

   _____

8. Chan will lend whoever needs them some mittens.

   _____

9. Elizabeth Taylor, who began her career in *National Velvet*, has always had starring roles. _____

10. Jamie will never work for a weapons manufacturer because he is deeply opposed to war. _____

11. Count Mondrian agreed to duel Prince Bacon at whatever time he wanted. _____

12. The man you are describing is my eccentric Uncle Pickles.

_____

13. Jeanette can always tell if I am pulling her leg.

_____

14. Corita's cat is bigger than her dog. _____

15. Whatever Mr. Moselle tells you is probably not true.

_____

16. The solution to this terrible crime is what I am seeking.

_____

17. Dawson City, which is located in Canada, was once a famous gold rush town. _____

18. While swimming, Lisa never eats pizza. _____

19. Isadora must go in whatever seems most appropriate.

_____

20. The Depression in the 1930s was a time when many people lost their jobs.

_____

E. *Directions:* Enclose each dependent clause in parentheses. Then indicate the function of each clause in the space provided at the end of the sentence.

S for subject	OP for object of the preposition
DO for direct object	ADJ for adjective
IO for indirect object	ADV for adverb
PN for predicate noun	

EXAMPLE: Bo plays the fiddle (whenever he can). ____ADV____

THE MISUNDERSTOOD BAT

1. Although they look like mice, bats are actually mammals.

_____

2. In fact, bats are the only mammals that are capable of true flight.

_____

3. Since they number between 1,000 and 2,000 species, there are millions of different kinds of bats in the world. _____

4. Studies show that bats are most abundant in the tropics. _____

5. That some bats migrate to warm places in the winter surprises most people. _____

6. Bats, whose bodies are furry and mouselike, vary greatly in size. _____

7. While some are less than one inch long, others grow as large as fifteen inches. _____

8. Bats' wings, which range from two inches to five feet, are extensions of the skin on their backs. _____

9. During the day bats hang upside down in whatever dark place is available. _____

10. Caves and buildings are where they generally like to sleep. _____

11. After they sleep all day, bats become active at night or twilight. _____

12. Most bats can see well, though they depend on echolocation (a kind of radar) to navigate in the dark.

13. Bats' diets, which include fruit, insects, small animals, and fish, vary greatly from species to species.

14. Why most people are afraid of bats is not clear. _____

15. The most probable reason is that South American vampire bats feed on the blood of living animals. _____

16. When people think of vampire bats, they are often reminded of the terrifying creature of legends. _____

17. Many people also fear that bats will give them rabies. _____

18. One common misconception is that bats will get tangled in people's hair. _____

19. Scientists who study bats defend this unpopular animal. _____

20. These scientists claim that bats are a useful and misunderstood mammal. _____

F. *Directions:* Write ten sentences of your own that contain noun clauses. Then enclose each noun clause in parentheses and indicate its function at the end of the sentence.

EXAMPLE: (What she sees in him) puzzles me.   subject

1. _____
2. _____
3. _____
4. _____
5. _____
6. _____
7. _____
8. _____
9. _____
10. _____

11. COMPLEX AND COMPOUND-COMPLEX SENTENCES

Are the following sentences simple or compound?

1. Since I started a doughnut shop, I have gained weight.
2. When I saw Mr. Lee, I asked him where he was going.
3. Jane listened to the story that her brother told the kids, but she didn't believe what he was saying.

If you read the title of this unit, you may have suspected that the question was a trick. The above sentences are neither simple nor compound. A simple sentence consists of one independent clause. A compound sentence, on the other hand, is two or more independent clauses joined by a coordinating conjunction. But if you look carefully at the sentences above, you'll discover that all three of them contain dependent clauses. What kinds of sentences are these?

Definition

Sentences are classified according to the number and kind of clauses they contain. There are four kinds of sentences: *simple, compound, complex,* and *compound-complex*. A **complex sentence** is a sentence that contains one independent clause and one or more dependent clauses. Sentences 1 and 2 are examples of complex sentences (the *dependent* clauses are in italics):

1. *Since I started a doughnut shop,* I have gained weight.
2. *When I saw Mr. Lee,* I asked him *where he was going.*

A **compound-complex sentence** is a sentence that contains two or more independent clauses and one or more dependent clauses. Sentence 3 is a good illustration of a compound-complex sentence (this time the *independent* clauses are in italics):

3. *Jane listened to the story* that her brother told the kids, but *she didn't believe* what he was saying.

USING SENTENCE VARIETY TO IMPROVE WRITING

Compound and compound-complex sentences give you more choice when you write. Although there is no one best kind of sentence, it is important to vary the length and type of sentences you use. If you use too many short, simple sentences, your writing will sound choppy and dull. If you use too many long compound-complex sentences, your writing will become confusing and your main ideas obscured. For example, read the following paragraph:

> Anita took the bus into town. She met her best friend, Susie. They walked around for an hour. They had a big fight. Anita walked away in tears. She took the bus home. She cried all the way. Anita sat in her room for some time. Then she called Susie on the phone. They said they were sorry. They made up. They are best friends again.

This paragraph may never be great literature. But by using subordination (dependent clauses) and varying the length and structure of sentences, you can improve the style and eliminate the monotony:

> Anita took the bus into town, where she met her best friend, Susie. After they walked around for an hour, they had a big fight. Anita walked away in tears. She took the bus home and cried all the way. Anita sat in her room for some time, but then she called Susie on the phone. Once they said they were sorry, they made up quickly. Now they are best friends again.

Compound and compound-complex sentences also allow you to relate one idea to another more precisely. For instance, you can express cause and effect clearly by using dependent clauses:

1. Because I won the lottery, I retired from my job.
2. After I got my degree, I received three job offers.

You can use dependent clauses to emphasize the exact point you want to make, too. When you say, "Although the movie was terrible, I had a nice evening," you are stressing the pleasant part of your experience. On the other hand, when you say, "Although I had a nice evening, the movie was terrible," you are emphasizing the less successful aspect of your night out. In general, it is a good idea to put the idea you wish to emphasize in the independent clause of a complex or compound-complex sentence.

Using compound and compound-complex sentences will help you to express your ideas more precisely. Varying the kinds of sentences you use will make your writing more interesting and effective, too.

COMPLEX AND COMPOUND-COMPLEX SENTENCE EXERCISES

A. *Directions:* Depending on what type of sentence it is, write *complex* or *compound-complex* in the space provided after each of the following sentences.

EXAMPLE: When Sid skis, he always catches a cold.
             complex

1. I never knew why Sally couldn't eat duck soup.

   _____

2. After he returned from school, Dale drank some milk, but he couldn't find the cookies. _____

3. The girl who won the award lives near the railroad station.

   _____

4. Erica always loved astronomy, and she discovered a comet when she was twelve. _____

5. Although Josie had never seen snow before, she knew how to make a snowball. _____

6. William Faulkner was a great writer, but he published books for years before he became famous. _____

7. Tony likes Cleo because she owns a beautiful boat.

   _____

8. Minnie didn't want to take the test, so she told her math teacher that she was sick. _____

9. Give me back my turtle, or I won't show you the snake I found under the sofa. _____

10. Mexico City, which has a population of more than 10 million people, is larger than New York City. _____

11. Nina looked as though she wanted to laugh, but she managed to restrain herself. _____

12. I'll sit here until the doctor arrives. _____

13. On a recent vacation Roberto explored the town where he was born. _____

14. Beulah is older than her brother, but she is still only three years old. _____

15. Although some people like liver, others wouldn't eat it if you paid them. _____

16. Mr. Metzger described a period of history when people were afraid of witches, and he asked the class to write reports on the subject. _____

17. Darlene likes avocados that are ripe, and she likes guacamole even better. _____

18. Mr. Langton, whose son climbed Mt. Everest, plays the trombone. _____

19. The senator missed the debate, but she voted after she met with the president. _____

20. What you plan to do interests me, but how will you get the money? _____

B. *Directions:* Depending on what type of sentence it is, write *simple, compound, complex,* or *compound-complex* in the space provided at the end of each sentence.

EXAMPLE: Peggy bought the gifts, and Biff wrapped them.
_____compound_____

ERIC BLAIR BECOMES GEORGE ORWELL

1. George Orwell was the pen-name of Eric Blair. _____

2. Orwell, whose parents were English, was born in India in 1903. _____

3. Richard Blair, Orwell's father, joined the British civil service in India in 1875. _____

4. When Orwell was four years old, his father took the family back to England, and they settled in Henley-on-Thames. _____

5. Orwell's older sister was named Marjorie, and his younger sister was named Avril. _____

6. Although Orwell was a bright child, he was also shy and quiet. _____

7. From a very early age, Orwell loved to read. _____

8. The Blairs sent their son to a boarding school when he turned eight. _____

9. Because he was close to his mother, Orwell did not want to go to school, and he hated his years at St. Cyprian's.

   _____

10. Orwell later wrote an essay about St. Cyprian's, "Such, Such Were the Joys." _____

11. After he left St. Cyprian's, Orwell attended Eton, an exclusive British "public" school. _____

12. At the age of 18, Orwell graduated from Eton, and he soon decided to join the British Imperial Police in India. _____

13. Although Orwell remained in India for five years, he quickly grew to hate the British rule over its colonies. _____

14. Orwell quit his job and returned to England in 1927.

   _____

15. Because he wanted to become a writer, he spent the next few years training himself to write. _____

16. He lived the life of a tramp on several occasions so that he could write a book about how the poor live. _____

17. This book, *Down and Out in Paris and London*, was published in 1933, and people began to take notice of Orwell.

   _____

18. Orwell liked to write novels, but he won more fame for the books that he wrote about English coal miners and the Spanish Civil War. _____

19. With the publication of *Animal Farm* in 1945, George Orwell became an internationally known writer. _____

20. Orwell's *1984* brought him even greater recognition, but his career was cut tragically short when he died of tuberculosis in 1950.

   _____

C. *Directions:* Rewrite each pair of sentences as either a *complex* or *compound-complex* sentence. Then enclose every dependent clause in parentheses. Be sure to punctuate your sentences correctly.

EXAMPLE: Gretta washed the car. Earlier she weeded the garden.
(Before Gretta washed the car), she weeded the garden.

1. Dr. Goldberg is a thoughtful person. She is my dentist.

   _____

2. Tammy caught a cold. She couldn't go to the slumber party.

   _____

3. The man is a famous writer, and he knows my mother. I saw the man yesterday.

   _____

4. Ahmad lost his ticket. The manager let him in to the movie.

   _____

5. Little Rock is the city. Michelle met her husband there.

   _____

6. The Taj Mahal is a breathtaking building. It is located in India.

   _____

7. Gigi participated in the demonstration, and she carried a sign. The sign read, "Help the homeless!"

   _____

8. Cara lost her cat. She has cried for days.

   _____

9. The murder mystery is suspenseful. I guessed the solution.

   _____

10. Muffie's sister lost her job, so she filed for unemployment. Then she landed a new job.

    _____

D. *Directions:* Insert the correct punctuation where it is needed in the following sentences. If no punctuation is needed, write *correct* at the end of the sentence.

EXAMPLE: After she cried, Ms. Moppet felt better.

1. Dirk played a wonderful game but Ruth played even better.
2. When Mindy finished the book she was sad so she started another one.
3. Jose and Juanita fetched a pail of water from the top of the hill.
4. Unless you plan to eat them all yourself share those doughnuts with me.
5. Because alligators are dangerous you must be careful in Florida or you could lose a limb.
6. Show me that picture again or I will never remember it.
7. My mom always checks the tire pressure before she goes on a long drive.
8. Pat almost jumped into the ocean but when she saw a shark she changed her mind.
9. Since Hiroshima was bombed in 1945 many people there have developed leukemia and a large percentage of those people have died.
10. The Kolchinskys and the Smiths drove to the beach and spent the afternoon there.
11. Although I often sleep late I am always tired.
12. Whenever Sue earns some money she buys a record and then she goes to Ruby's house and plays it.

E. *Directions:* Following the sentence types indicated below, write ten complex and compound-complex sentences of your own. Then enclose all the dependent clauses in parentheses.

EXAMPLE: complex   (After he lost), Al felt miserable.

1. complex

_____

2. compound-complex

_____

3. complex

_____

4. complex

_____

5. compound-complex

_____

6. compound-complex

_____

7. complex

_____

8. compound-complex

_____

9. complex

_____

10. compound-complex

_____

12. INTRODUCTION TO VERBALS

Each of the following sentences contains an italicized word or words. Can you identify the parts of speech of these words?

1. *Singing* is Octavia's favorite hobby.
2. The *growling* dog scared the mail carrier.
3. Sam seemed afraid *to talk*.

If you answered that all of the italicized words are verbs, you are partly right. *Singing*, *growling*, and *to talk* are all formed from verbs, and all three convey a sense of action. In the above sentences, however, *singing* is a noun, *growling* is an adjective, and *to talk* is an adverb.

Definition

The words *singing, growling,* and *to talk*, as they are used in the above sentences, are all examples of verbals. A **verbal** is a word that is formed from a verb but functions as a noun, an adjective, or an adverb. There are three kinds of verbals: **gerunds**, which function as nouns; **participles**, which function as adjectives; and **infinitives**, which function as nouns, adjectives, or adverbs.

People sometimes have trouble telling the difference between verbals and the main verb of a sentence. See if you can recognize the difference. Read the following sentences carefully. Then underline the main verbs twice and circle the verbals:

1. Swimming the English Channel quickly is difficult.
2. Swimming slowly, the elephant won the race.
3. Harold loves to swim daily.

The main verbs of these sentences are the words *is*, *won*, and *loves*. The words *Swimming* (gerund/noun), *Swimming* (participle/adjective), and *to swim* (infinitive/noun) are the verbals.

Although they function as nouns, adjectives, and adverbs, verbals *do* act like verbs in some ways. Apart from showing action, they also have modifiers and take objects. In the sentences above, for instance, *English Channel* is the object of the gerund *Swimming*, and the adverb *slowly* modifies the participle *Swimming*. Similarly, the adverb *daily* modifies the infinitive *to swim*.

HINT A verbal can never take the place of a main verb. Any group of words that contains a verbal, but no main verb, is a sentence fragment.

1. *To go* to the movies (fragment)
2. The *flying* geese (fragment)
3. *To go* to the movies is my idea of a good time. (sentence)
4. The *flying* geese turned to the south. (sentence)

13. GERUNDS

After underlining the nouns in the following sentences, answer the questions in the spaces provided:

1. Rowing a boat tires your arms.

   What is the subject of this sentence? _____

2. Bernie's best friend loves skiing.

   What is the direct object of this sentence? _____

3. By playing fairly, Josie won her classmates' admiration.

   What is the object of the preposition in this sentence?

   _____

If you said *Rowing* is the subject of sentence 1, *skiing* is the direct object of sentence 2, and *playing* is the object of the preposition in sentence 3, you're absolutely right. Did you notice anything else about these words? Yes, all three end in *-ing*, but what else? Although all three of these words are functioning as nouns, you may have realized that all three were formed from verbs.

> **Definition**
>
> The words *Running*, *skiing*, and *playing* in the above sentences are all examples of gerunds. A **gerund** is a word ending in *-ing* that is formed from a verb and used as a noun. Like other nouns, gerunds may be used as subjects, direct objects, indirect objects, predicate nouns, appositives, and objects of the preposition.

1. *Working* hard is not my idea of fun. (subject)
2. I like *reading* long books on rainy days. (direct object)
3. Emilio gave *studying* his complete attention. (indirect object)
4. Ruth's favorite pastime was *singing* loudly in the shower. (predicate noun)
5. Roland's new hobby, *stargazing*, must be done at night. (appositive)
6. What are Zuni's chances of *winning* the lottery? (object of the preposition)

Now try writing some sentences of your own that contain gerunds. Can you identify the functions of these gerunds?

MODIFIERS AND OBJECTS

Although they function as nouns, gerunds retain some of the characteristics of verbs. In a sense, they are *verb-like nouns*. In addition to conveying a sense of action, gerunds have modifiers and take objects. To understand this idea, look back at the six sentences above. The adverb *hard* in sentence 1 modifies the gerund *working*, just as the adverb *loudly* in sentence 4 modifies the gerund *singing*. On the other hand, the noun *books* in sentence 2 is the direct object of the gerund *reading*, and the noun *shower* in sentence 4 is the object of the preposition of the gerund *singing*.

USING THE POSSESSIVE BEFORE A GERUND

Always use the possessive form of a noun or pronoun before a gerund:

1. The teacher did not understand Sally's (not Sally) finishing the test early.
2. Uncle Carl disapproves of his (*not* him) listening to rock music all day.

If you think about it, you'll see why this rule makes sense. In sentence 1, for instance, it's not a question of the teacher's not understanding *Sally*; rather, it's a question of her not understanding *Sally's finishing the test early*. Similarly, Uncle Carl does not disapprove of the person himself; he disapproves of *his listening to rock music all day*.

HINT Although gerunds do act like verbs in some ways, it is important to remember that they function as nouns and are considered to be nouns.

GERUND EXERCISES

A. *Directions:* Underline the gerunds in the following sentences. Then write the function of each gerund in the space provided at the end of the sentence. Remember that gerunds may be used as subjects, direct objects, indirect objects, predicate nouns, appositives, and objects of the preposition.
EXAMPLE: <u>Talking</u> is easy to do. _____subject_____

1. Hiking tests your endurance in several ways.

   _____

2. Frank enjoyed riding in the desert last summer.

   _____

3. Mr. Mcgraw's favorite sport is wrestling. _____

4. The baby was not very good at changing her own diapers.

   _____

5. Bev's hobby, collecting butterflies, kept her busy.

   _____

6. Leading a quiet life was not Eleanor Roosevelt's cup of tea.

   _____

7. Chang's main goal in life is beating his sister at checkers.

   _____

8. After playing records all evening, Ariadne had a terrible headache.

   _____

9. Rex could not forgive Shirley's refusing his invitation.

   _____

10. Cory gave daydreaming a bad name.   _____

11. Cutting the mustard in Montana is hard work.

   _____

12. Samuel Johnson liked living in London best of all.

   _____

13. They talked for hours before discovering they were cousins.

   _____

14. Herbert's latest habit was scratching his head.

   _____

15. At the tolling of the bell, Mr. Donne looked at his watch and frowned.   _____

16. William Faulkner disliked leaving his home in Oxford, Mississippi.   _____

17. Freezing on top of a mountain is not Gretchen's idea of fun.

   _____

18. The book's main subject, canoeing, fascinated Lou.

   _____

19. The thought of breaking the record thrilled Bob.

   _____

20. Another fun activity is catching lizards in jars.

   _____

B. *Directions:* Underline the gerunds in the following sentences. Then write the function of each gerund in the space provided at the end of the sentence.

EXAMPLE: Jean likes <u>walking</u> in the country. <u> direct object </u>

WHERE TO FIND BIZARRE FACTS

1. Tracking down bizarre facts is not easy. _____

2. You must love sitting in libraries for long hours. _____

3. You must also be skilled at finding the right books. _____

4. An important first step is acquiring good library skills. _____

5. Knowing the card catalog and its uses is essential. _____

6. If you have not done it before, give searching through the drawers in the catalog a try. _____

7. You probably could not help noticing the subject cards. _____

8. The purpose of these cards is informing you of the contents of the subsequent cards. _____

9. By looking through the cards on "Hobbies," for instance, you can locate all the books on various types of hobbies. _____

10. One hobby, collecting stamps for example, might have more entries in the catalog than other hobbies. _____

11. While you search through these cards, you might try investigating a book about a strange hobby. _____

12. Perhaps painting sharks' teeth is a hobby in some parts of the world. _____

13. One byproduct of using a card catalog, then, is that you often stumble across interesting books. _____

14. One way to achieve your goal, locating bizarre facts, would be to find a subject card on "Trivia" or "Strange Events." _____

15. Another good way to discover weird facts is browsing in an encyclopedia. _____

16. Coming across strange objects in an encyclopedia is not unusual. _____

17. Try reading the entries about more normal subjects, too. _____

18. By skimming an article about sharks, you would learn that sharks must move constantly or die. _____

19. Going to a library, then, could help to make your search productive. _____

20. Ripley probably began his first *Believe It or Not* book by thumbing through a card catalog or encyclopedia. _____

C. *Directions:* Underline the gerunds in the following sentences. Then label each gerund's modifiers and objects.

   ADJ for adjective   DO for direct object
   ADV for adverb   OP for object of the preposition

                  DO   ADV

EXAMPLE: <u>Finding</u> the answer quickly is not always possible.

1. Mr. Jordan loves hiking in the Dolomites.
2. Breathing deeply before a test calms Ashley's nerves.
3. Sidney's only achievement is catching flies.
4. Dabney's hopes of watching television quietly were shattered.
5. Breaking the record convincingly was Beryl's goal.
6. How do you feel about Bill's cheating at cards?
7. The girls enjoy working hard around the farm.
8. Ray's only hope is changing the teacher's mind immediately.
9. Asking a person politely can make all the difference.
10. I was surprised at his protecting the criminal from the police.

D. *Directions:* Circle the form of the noun or pronoun that should be used in each of the following sentences.

EXAMPLE: (Bill/Bill's) running away surprised us.

1. Chip was amazed by (Amy's/Amy) winning the prize.
2. Mona dislikes (me/my) talking on the phone.
3. I appreciated (your/you) speaking up for me yesterday.
4. (Bert/Bert's) refusing to play saddened me.
5. None of us agreed to (Timothy's/Timothy) taking the best piece of cake.
6. Many Americans disapproved of our (country/country's) getting involved in the Vietnam War.
7. We all enjoyed (Shirley's/Shirley) retelling the story.
8. (Maya's/Maya) studying for the big test paid off.
9. Did you hear about (Curly/Curly's) escaping the alligator?
10. Brad was angered at (Chan/Chan's) forgetting the tickets.
11. (Hansel's/Hansel) wandering in the woods worried Gretel.
12. Leonard adored (Wanda/Wanda's) dancing.
13. Bea was heartbroken by the (college's/college) deciding to reject her.
14. Tory applauded (Herb's/Herb) cutting down on coffee.
15. (Renaldo/Renaldo's) missing the dress rehearsal didn't please the director.

E. *Directions:* Rewrite each pair of sentences as one sentence using a gerund.

EXAMPLE: Chet blinked twice. Then he said, "Goodnight, David."
After blinking twice, Chet said, "Goodnight, David."

1. I do not like to iron my clothes. It is a big bore.

   _____

2. Mom threw away the lottery ticket. As a result, she lost a fortune.

   _____

3. You must choose a career. It is an important decision.

   _____

4. Hazel never read books. The very thought horrified her.

   _____

5. My older brother yelled at me. He apologized to me later.

   _____

6. They played a song by the Beatles. It caught everyone's attention.

   _____

7. Lola liked to skip rocks across ponds. She liked to do it every day.

   _____

8. This course has a purpose. The purpose is to teach people to climb trees.

   _____

9. Malcolm fixed the car himself. That is what gave him new confidence.

   _____

10. Mr. Bisby looked carefully at the money. Then he picked it up.

   _____

F. *Directions:* Write ten sentences of your own that contain gerunds. Then underline each gerund and indicate its function at the end of the sentence.

   EXAMPLE: <u>Sneezing</u> is not fun.   subject

   1. _____
   2. _____
   3. _____
   4. _____
   5. _____
   6. _____
   7. _____
   8. _____
   9. _____
   10. _____

14. PARTICIPLES

Underline the adjectives in the following sentences. (Don't underline articles.) Then write the word each adjective modifies in the space provided at the end of the sentence:

1. The creeping vine soon covered the wall. _____
2. Moving quietly, Horace followed the spy. _____
3. Tarzan stepped over the fallen tree. _____
4. Confused by the noise, the man didn't hear the announcement.

   _____

If you underlined the words *creeping, moving, fallen,* and *confused,* you identified the adjectives correctly. Now what do you notice about these adjectives? You may already have noticed that all of these adjectives convey a sense of action and that all of them were formed from verbs. Despite their verb-like qualities, however, these four words function as adjectives and modify the words *vine, Horace, tree,* and *man.*

Definition
The words *creeping, moving, fallen,* and *confused* in the above sentences are all examples of participles. A **participle** is a word that is formed from a verb and used as an adjective. Like other adjectives, participles modify nouns and pronouns. A participle must appear near the word it modifies.

EXAMPLE: Wearing a new skirt, Mary went to the concert with Georgio.
NOT: Mary went to the concert with Georgio wearing a new skirt.

There are two forms of participles: present participles and past participles. **Present participles** end in *-ing* (*racing, laughing, boring*). **Past participles** end in *-ed, -d, -t, -en,* and *-n* (*charmed, freed, slept, bitten, driven*); however, the past participles of certain verbs are formed by changing a vowel (*begin/begun, ring/rung, sink/sunk*). In the sentences above, *creeping* and *moving* are present participles, whereas *fallen* and *confused* are past participles.

Like gerunds, participles have modifiers and take objects. Underline the participles in the following sentences. Then label the words that modify these participles and the objects the participles take:

1. The fire grew stronger, heating the room slowly.
2. Raising her hand quickly, Beth caught the baseball.

In sentence 1 the adverb *slowly* modifies the participle *heating*, while the noun *room* is the direct object of that participle. The adverb *quickly* modifies the participle *raising* in sentence 2, and the direct object of that participle is the noun *hand*.

USING PARTICIPLES IN TWO WAYS

A participle may be used either as an adjective or as part of a verb phrase. When used with a helping verb, a participle is considered to be part of the main verb of a clause:

1. The *sleeping* bear suddenly woke up. (adjective)
2. The bear *is sleeping* in the cave. (main verb)
3. *Laughing* loudly, the man left the restaurant. (adjective)
4. A man *is laughing* somewhere in this restaurant. (main verb)

Remember that the participle in a verb phrase is part of the verb, not an adjective modifying the subject. Most participles, however, are used as adjectives.

PUNCTUATION

Always use a comma after a participle that begins a sentence:

1. *Puzzled*, Dave asked Professor Blimpkins to explain the problem.
2. *Screaming* loudly, the tax collectors tried to escape the mob.
3. *Walking* slowly down the street, Jessica spotted a dollar bill.

Notice that the comma appears *after* a participle's modifiers and/or objects.

HINTS

A. If you're not sure which word a participle modifies, just ask yourself the question *Who?* or *What?* about the participle:

1. Whispering softly, the mother quieted the frightened child.
2. A wounded tiger, roaring loudly, chased me up a tree.

In sentence 1, for instance, who is whispering? The answer to this question—*mother*—is the noun that the participle *whispering* is modifying. Using the same strategy, ask yourself what is roaring in sentence 2. When you answer that the *tiger* is roaring, you'll have discovered which word the participle *roaring* modifies.

B. Be careful not to confuse the present participle with the gerund, which has the same form but is used—as you know—as a noun:

1. *Sleeping* is Bert's favorite hobby. (gerund)
2. It is best to let *sleeping* dogs lie. (participle)

C. When you are writing sentences with participles, make sure that the participle clearly and sensibly modifies a word in the sentence. If it doesn't, you have probably used a dangling participle in your sentence:

1. Hiking in the Rockies, Leah's ankle was broken.
2. Jethro saw a monkey driving his car down the street.

Sentence 1 implies that Leah's ankle was hiking in the Rockies. Sentence 2 implies that a monkey was driving Jethro's car. To avoid dangling participles like these, make sure it is clear which word in the sentence the participle is modifying. You can usually accomplish this goal by placing the word the participle modifies *directly after* the comma when a participle begins a sentence:

1. Hiking in the Rockies, Leah broke her ankle.
2. Driving his car down the street, Jethro saw a monkey.

PARTICIPLE EXERCISES

A. *Directions:* Underline the participles in the following sentences. Then write the word each participle modifies in the space at the end of the sentence.

EXAMPLE: <u>Dancing</u> fleas are unusual. _____fleas_____

1. Murphy reacted to the exciting news with a smile.

   _____

2. Whistling cheerfully, Brent strolled into work.

   _____

3. The man napping on the beach did not see the tidal wave.

   _____

4. Ridden the wrong way, a motorcycle can be dangerous.

   _____

5. The falling leaves filled Jane with sadness. _____

6. Miss Marple, baffled by the lack of evidence in the murder case, went on a holiday. _____

7. Invading Russia without warning, Hitler stunned Stalin.

   _____

8. The river looks lovely, shining like diamonds in the bright sun.

   _____

9. Seen for the first time, the northern lights can take your breath away. _____

10. The melting snowman started to cry. _____

11. Lurking beneath the surface, the Loch Ness Monster waited for lunch. _____

12. The bread, baked for two hours in a hot oven, was black as ashes.

    _____

13. Jennifer soaked her frozen feet in warm water.

    _____

14. Feeling silly, Mel put on the duck costume. _____

15. The birds, chirping loudly outside, woke me up.

    _____

16. Lurching from side to side, the truck ground to a halt.

    _____

17. The sunken boat contained a treasure chest. _____

18. Longing to be home again, Reed wrote a long letter to his parents.

    _____

19. Caught by an enormous lizard, the boy was never seen again.

    _____

20. The bird hanging from the pear tree was a partridge.

    _____

B. *Directions:* Underline the participles in the following sentences. Then write the word each participle modifies in the space provided at the end of the sentence.

   EXAMPLE: That goose is a <u>sitting</u> duck. _____duck_____

RUDYARD KIPLING

1. Rudyard Kipling, born in Bombay in 1865, spent his early years in India. _____

2. The reigning English monarch for much of Kipling's early life was Queen Victoria. _____

3. Wanting a good education for their son, Kipling's parents sent him to a school in England. _____

4. Racked by homesickness, Kipling hated his harsh guardians in England. _____

5. Kipling developed his writing talents at school.
_____

6. Finishing his studies in 1882, Kipling returned to India the same year. _____

7. Hoping to become a writer, he joined the staff of a newspaper.
_____

8. Kipling's first book, *Departmental Ditties*, contained biting satires on the Indian Civil Service. _____

9. Building on this early success, Kipling published two volumes of short stories in 1888. _____

10. Stopping to explore America on the way, Kipling traveled back to London in 1889. _____

11. Comfortably settled in England, Kipling wrote *Barrackroom Ballads*, a collection of poems. _____

12. Kipling married an American in 1892 and spent the next four years in Vermont, known for its peaceful and pastoral beauty.
_____

13. Kipling, enjoying his most productive years, wrote *Captains Courageous* and his two *Jungle Books* in Vermont. _____

14. In 1899, living once again in England, Kipling lost his beloved daughter. _____

15. *Kim*, considered Kipling's best story by some, appeared in 1901.
_____

16. In 1907, crowning his already considerable achievement, Kipling won the Nobel Prize for literature. _____

17. This glowing tribute marked the end of his best work.
_____

18. Shattered by the death of his only son during World War I, Kipling became a bitter, lonely man in his later years.
_____

19. Many people, disturbed by his support of British imperialism, have criticized Kipling's poems and stories. _____

20. *Kim* and the *Jungle Books*, Kipling's best remembered works, are still very popular with children. _____

C. *Directions:* Underline the participles in the following sentences. Then label each participle's modifiers and objects.

ADV for adverb   OP for object of the preposition
DO for direct object

EXAMPLE: <u>Bending</u> quickly, Rhonda sprained her back.

1. Holding the cup carefully, Jack followed Jill up the hill.
2. The dog, scared by the loud noise, whined pitifully.
3. The bowl of flowers sat near the window, glowing brilliantly in the afternoon sun.
4. Raising her arms slowly, Zelda tapped her baton and looked at the band.
5. The creature scuttling swiftly along the sand is a hermit crab.
6. Grinning nastily, the bully pulled June's pigtails again.
7. Mr. Bentley, angered by the noise, called the police.
8. Pulling the rabbit out of his hat, the magician turned and vanished.
9. The tall woman speaking to my mother lives in a tree house.
10. Sniffing the air suspiciously, Cal asked what we were having for dinner.

D. *Directions:* Underline the participles in the following sentences. If the participle is functioning as an adjective, write **adjective** in the space provided at the end of the sentence. If the participle is part of a verb phrase, write **verb** in the space provided.
EXAMPLE: The mouse was <u>running</u> from the cat. _____verb_____

1. Sparkling brightly, the snow blinded the fur trapper.

_____

2. The road runner threw a shoe at the howling coyote.

   _____

3. Lorraine was hurrying home when the tornado hit.

   _____

4. Momentarily lost, Hank asked a stranger for directions.

   _____

5. Before she moved here, Ms. Topaz was working at a famous university. _____

6. The package of secret papers was sitting at the airport.

   _____

7. The slithering snake vanished like lightning. _____

8. Overjoyed by the good news, Marlene had a party.

   _____

9. The man in the red hat was lying. _____

10. The squirting water completely drenched the unsuspecting businesspeople. _____

11. The eighteenth century manor was burning to the ground.

    _____

12. Turning sharply to the right, the border collie herded the stray sheep back into the flock. _____

E. *Directions:* Rewrite each of the following sentences using a participle. Be sure to punctuate your sentences correctly.

   EXAMPLE: The girls shivered from the cold and waved madly at the plane.
   Shivering from the cold, the girls waved madly at the plane.

   1. Mom unbuttoned her coat and began giving orders.

      _____

   2. The tax form confused Mr. Halperin, so he sent it to his accountant.

      _____

   3. The geese landed on the lake and started to quack loudly.

      _____

   4. The loud noise frightened the chipmunk, and it ran away.

      _____

5. Prince Charming hacked his way through the forest and found the silent castle.

_____

6. Gerald watched the news, and at the same time he sewed up his pants.

_____

7. Newton sat under an apple tree and accidentally discovered gravity.

_____

8. Gwendolyn extended her hands and tiptoed across the tightrope.

_____

9. Larry walked home slowly, and he thought about Patty the whole time.

_____

10. Val caught the ball and threw it back to the pitcher.

_____

F. *Directions:* Underline the verbals in the following sentences. Then indicate whether they are **gerunds** or **participles** in the spaces provided.
EXAMPLE: <u>Carrying</u> buckets of water can hurt your arms.
_____gerund_____

1. Wallowing in the mud, the pig grunted with joy.

_____

2. I chose fencing as my winter activity. _____

3. The raging tornado destroyed the bowling alley.

_____

4. My sister would not give driving another chance.

_____

5. Hoping for peace, Neville Chamberlain returned to England.

_____

6. Mr. Higgins, disturbed by his students' bad work habits, left for Europe. _____

7. Uncle Randolph's one fault, sleeping at the dinner table, was minor. _____

8. Shamir listened to the sound of the whispering brook.

   _____

9. The doorman's only job is opening the hotel door.

   _____

10. Boarding the train, Cousin Bea turned to wave goodbye.

    _____

11. The idea of joining a circus appealed to Sophie.

    _____

12. Senator Wingate, slipping steadily in the polls, withdrew from the race. _____

13. Hunting vampires in Transylvania can be a dangerous experience.

    _____

14. The grinning clown looked strangely sinister.

    _____

15. The yellow dog walked toward me, hobbling badly the entire way.

    _____

16. You have no real reason for returning this gift.

    _____

17. Elena's nightly activity, walking in the moonlight, was not always safe. _____

18. Writhing in pain, the fallen soldier clutched his leg.

    _____

19. The baby's constant crying drove me crazy. _____

20. The cat almost ate the incredible shrinking man.

    _____

G. *Directions:* Write ten sentences of your own that contain participles. Then underline each participle and write the word it modifies at the end of the sentence.
   EXAMPLE: <u>Arriving</u> at the dance, Brenda saw her friends.   Brenda

   1. _____
   2. _____
   3. _____
   4. _____
   5. _____

6. _____

7. _____

8. _____

9. _____

10. _____

H. *Directions:* Write five sentences of your own that contain dangling participles. Then rewrite each sentence correctly.

EXAMPLE: Howling at the moon, I listened to the dog.
I listened to the dog howling at the moon.

1. _____

_____

2. _____

_____

3. _____

_____

4. _____

_____

5. _____

_____

15. INFINITIVES

Read the following sentences carefully. After each sentence write the function of the italicized words in the space provided. Treat each pair of italicized words as one unit or item:

1. *To succeed* means everything. _____
2. The place *to visit* is Mexico. _____
3. The people came *to see* the game. _____

If you are having trouble figuring out the functions of these words, think about what role they are playing in each sentence. For instance, in sentence 1, *To succeed* is doing the action of the verb *means*; therefore, it is a noun and the subject of the sentence. In sentence 2, on the other hand, *to visit* gives you more information about the noun *place*. It tells you that Mexico is the place *to visit*, not the place *to avoid*; therefore, *to visit* is modifying a noun and is an adjective in this sentence. In sentence 3, finally, *to see* gives you more information about the verb *came*. It tells you *why* the people came—*to see* the game, not *to boo* it; therefore, *to see* is modifying a verb and is an adverb in this sentence.

> **Definition**
> The italicized pairs of words in the above sentences are all examples of infinitives. An **infinitive** is a form of the verb, usually preceded by the word *to*, that is used as a noun, an adjective, or an adverb. Infinitives are most commonly used as nouns. Like nouns, they function as subjects, direct objects, predicate nouns, and objects of the preposition.

1. *To learn* Russian quickly is difficult. (subject)
2. Al wanted *to buy* the car immediately. (direct object)
3. Joyce's big dream is *to visit* Disneyland. (predicate noun)
4. Melony was not about *to stop* now. (object of the preposition)

Infinitives sometimes function as adjectives and adverbs as well:

5. Ruby told him the castles *to see* in England. (adjective)
6. Maureen went *to visit* her mother yesterday. (adverb)
7. The attempt *to demolish* the school failed. (adjective)
8. *To understand* the problem completely, Caitlin asked a question. (adverb)

Like gerunds and participles, infinitives can have modifiers and take objects. For example, in sentences 1 and 2 above, the adverbs *quickly* and *immediately* modify the infinitives *to learn* and *to buy*. Similarly, in sentences 6 and 7 the words *mother* and *school* are the direct objects of the infinitives *to visit* and *to demolish*. See if you can find other examples in these sentences of words that are modifying or serving as the direct objects of infinitives.

Be careful not to confuse the infinitive, which is a verbal beginning with *to*, with prepositional phrases that begin with *to*:

9. I would love *to see* your house. (infinitive)
10. Let's go *to your house*. (prepositional phrase)

Remember that infinitives consist of *to* followed by a verb, whereas prepositional phrases consist of *to* followed by a noun or pronoun.

OMITTING *TO*

The sign of the infinitive, the word *to*, may be omitted after certain verbs:

1. Mr. Broderick helped *vacuum* the house.
2. Let me *give* this to Bert.
3. My sister saw me *buy* the chocolate.

Although they are not preceded by *to*, the words *vacuum*, *give*, and *buy* are all infinitives. The word *to* is often omitted after the following verbs: *dare, feel, hear, help, let, make, need, see,* and *watch*.

PUNCTUATION

If an infinitive comes at the beginning of a sentence and functions as an adverb, insert a comma after it:

1. *To recover*, he stayed in bed.
2. *To rob* the bank, Jesse James needed a horse.
3. *To row* the boat quickly, Stan pulled harder on the oars.

Be sure to insert the comma *after* an introductory infinitive's modifiers and objects.

HINTS

A. In general, sentences sound less awkward if you do not split infinitives. A **split infinitive** contains an adverb between the word *to* and the verb. It is usually better to place the adverb somewhere else in the sentence:

1. Brady wanted *to slowly read* the paper. (split infinitive)
2. Brady wanted *to read* the paper slowly. (infinitive not split)

Sometimes a sentence will sound more awkward if you do not split an infinitive. In these cases insert the adverb between the word *to* and the verb:

1. He seemed *to suddenly lose* his nerve.
2. The sparks caused her *to just shut* her eyes.

B. It is sometimes difficult to tell the difference between infinitives that are functioning as direct objects and infinitives that are functioning as adverbs:

1. Ada loves *to play* marbles. (direct object)
2. Ada ran *to tell* her mother. (adverb)

If an infinitive is a direct object, it should answer the direct object question *What?* For example, if you ask yourself, "Ada loves what?" the answer is the infinitive *to play*. If, on the other hand, you ask yourself, "Ada ran what?" the infinitive *to tell* is not the answer. Rather, the infinitive *to tell* lets you know *why* Ada ran to her mother; it functions as an adverb.

C. Adjectival infinitives almost always follow immediately after the nouns or pronouns they modify. Adverbial infinitives may appear either before or after the verbs they modify:

1. The team *to see* is the Rebels. (adjective)
2. Rita came *to hear* the speech. (adverb)
3. *To buy* the tickets, Tim spent all his savings. (adverb)

INFINITIVE EXERCISES

A. *Directions:* Underline the infinitives in the following sentences. Then, depending on the function of the infinitive, write **noun**, **adjective**, or **adverb** in the space provided at the end of each sentence.
EXAMPLE: *To err* is human. _____noun_____

1. Thomas learned to tie his shoes today. _____

2. To paint pictures on pins requires steady hands.

   _____

3. Roberta came to meet the president. _____

4. Abraham Lincoln's main goal was to save the Union.

   _____

5. The time to state your opinion is over. _____

6. When I called, Tess was about to write me a letter.

   _____

7. To catch a horse, you must have a rope. _____

8. Sim expected to find his parents at home. _____

9. To learn the name of his benefactor was Pip's goal.

_____

10. Alaska is a good place to find bears. _____

11. Martin Luther King's aim was to win freedom for his people.

_____

12. Elvida came to the city to find a job. _____

13. The chance to win an important role does not appear every day.

_____

14. Stephen Biko wanted to abolish the system of apartheid in South

Africa. _____

15. The really important thing is to have a good time.

_____

16. To catch the tiger, Ms. Perkins set a trap. _____

17. Help me find a job in publishing. _____

18. The urge to eat the goldfish overwhelmed him.

_____

19. Gabriel waited to see the elephant's next move.

_____

20. Raji hoped to change his father's mind. _____

B. *Directions:* Underline the infinitives in the following sentences. Then write the function of each infinitive in the space provided at the end of the sentence.

S for the subject	OP for object of the preposition
DO for direct object	ADJ for adjective
PN for predicate noun	ADV for adverb

EXAMPLE: Chuck expects *to hear* from her on Tuesday.
_____DO_____

1. To invent the first telephone was Alexander Graham Bell's aim.

_____

2. Susan B. Anthony believed that all women should have the right

to vote. _____

3. Charles Lindbergh's dream was to fly across the Atlantic alone.

   _____

4. Neil Armstrong rode in a space capsule to get to the moon.

   _____

5. Margaret Mead wanted to introduce people to new cultures.

   _____

6. The mountain to climb, in Edmund Hillary's view, was Mt. Everest. _____

7. When she died, Charlotte Bronte was about to have her first child.

   _____

8. James Madison wrote essays to persuade people that the United States Constitution should be ratified. _____

9. Jonas Salk hoped to rid the world of polio with his new vaccine.

   _____

10. To rescue black people from slavery was Harriet Tubman's goal.

    _____

11. The best book to read about the dangers of pesticides is Rachel Carson's *Silent Spring*. _____

12. Chief Joseph's hope was to escape to Canada with his tribe.

    _____

13. John Steinbeck wrote *The Grapes of Wrath* to show the plight of the migrant worker in the 1930s. _____

14. At an early age Emily Dickinson decided to write poetry.

    _____

15. When she was about to stop writing, Barbara Pym's work was rediscovered. _____

16. The person to reach the South Pole first was Roald Amundsen.

    _____

17. To expose the Watergate scandal was Bob Woodward and Carl Bernstein's desire. _____

18. Adolf Hitler's intention was to conquer the world.

    _____

19. During Richard Nixon's presidency the states amended the Constitution to give eighteen-year-olds voting rights.

    _____

20. Elizabeth Gurley Flynn helped organize industrial workers into labor unions before World War I. _____

C. *Directions:* Underline the infinitives in the following sentences. Then label each infinitive's modifiers and objects.

> ADV for adverb   OP for object of the preposition
> DO for direct object

EXAMPLE: Binkley hates <u>to read</u> long books slowly.
(DO above "books", ADV above "slowly")

1. To eat chocolate daily is Miguel's dream.
2. The place to go for fun is Antigua.
3. Professor Mandella is about to leave the country forever.
4. I opened the album to show the pictures to my friend.
5. Leslie intended to wash her car yesterday.
6. "The best island to see in Greece is Corfu," Ron said.
7. Her intention is to write the great American novel someday.
8. To rise rapidly through the ranks is Gregory's only concern.
9. The candidate hopes to win the mayor's endorsement soon.
10. Priscilla entered the contest to win a car for her mother.

D. *Directions:* Rewrite each of the following sentences to eliminate the split infinitive.
EXAMPLE: Jane expects to quickly find a job.
        Jane expects to find a job quickly.

1. Reginald hopes to soon hear the results of the test.

   _____

2. My goal is to eventually replace my old stereo system.

   _____

3. To clearly defend her position was Maria's wish.

   _____

4. The police officer had to carefully analyze the situation.

   _____

5. David likes to regularly play tennis.

   _____

6. Gail decided to immediately memorize the poem.

_____

7. To better see the board, Kristen moved to the front of the class-room.

_____

8. It is illegal to wrongfully accuse someone of a crime.

_____

9. Edwina was forced to loudly call out my name.

_____

10. To effectively fix a car, you need good tools.

_____

E. *Directions:* Rewrite the following sentences, using infinitives to make them more concise.

EXAMPLE: I gave a party so that I could meet my new neighbor.
I gave a party to meet my new neighbor.

1. Midnight is the time when you should go home.

_____

2. Mr. Smith bought a castle in order that he impress his neighbors.

_____

3. The man decided that he should solve his own problems.

_____

4. Hortense painted the room purple so that its appearance would be improved.

_____

5. In order that she might increase her score on the test, Lori studied day and night.

_____

6. Leroy walked the other way because he felt that he should avoid trouble.

_____

7. Harriet Tubman risked her life so that she could help Blacks escape slavery.

_____

8. In order that you hear everything I say, sit close to the front.

   _____

9. It is more dangerous if you skydive without a parachute.

   _____

10. Because she thought that she would make herself feel better, Mary Lou confessed.

    _____

F. *Directions:* Underline each of the verbals in the following sentences. Then indicate whether it is a **gerund**, **participle**, or **infinitive** in the space provided at the end of the sentence.
   EXAMPLE: The <u>freezing</u> camper built a fire. _____participle_____

ARTHUR RANSOME

1. Born in 1884, Arthur Ransome grew up in Leeds, England.

   _____

2. Ransome loved to go to the Lake District for his summer holiday.

   _____

3. Exploring the countryside around the lakes was Ransome's favorite pastime. _____

4. The towering, rugged hills sparked his imagination.

   _____

5. To leave the lakes behind at summer's end was more than Ransome could bear. _____

6. Ransome's dream was to live there all year. _____

7. Ransome's first career, publishing, did not hold his interest very long. _____

8. In order to become a writer, Ransome quit his job with a London publisher. _____

9. Ransome succeeded in publishing his first book in 1906 at the age of 22. _____

10. For the next several years Ransome continued to write books.

    _____

11. Seeking new adventures, Ransome traveled in Russia for several years. _____

12. He found many stories to include in his book on Russian folk tales. _____

13. Ransome started writing newspaper articles while he was in Russia. _____

14. He covered the exciting events of the 1917 Russian Revolution for the *Manchester Guardian*. _____

15. Ransome still believed that the best place to be was the Lake District. _____

16. To fulfill his dream, he retired and bought a house there in 1929. _____

17. Drawing on his childhood memories, Ransome wrote *Swallows and Amazons* the next year. _____

18. The novel is about a group of young people who love to spend their summer holidays in the Lake District. _____

19. The favorite hobby of these children is sailing. _____

20. Settled happily in his favorite place, Ransome wrote many more adventure books about the Lake District. _____

G. *Directions:* Underline the verbals in the following sentences. Then label each one as **gerund** (GER), **participle** (PAR), or **infinitive** (INF), and indicate its function in the space provided at the end of the sentence.

S for subject	APP for appositive
DO for direct object	OP for object of the preposition
IO for indirect object	ADJ for adjective
PN for predicate noun	ADV for adverb

GER
EXAMPLE: I teach bowling every Sunday night. _____ DO _____

1. Building sand castles is Marvin's favorite activity. _____

2. Edgar Allan Poe wrote dozens of frightening short stories. _____

3. Bruce loves to eat clams in the summer. _____

4. Donna's hobby, diving, can be dangerous. _____

5. Shivering with cold, Simon pulled on his mittens.

_____

6. To lie seems usually like a poor solution. _____

7. Sammy saved the people by shouting a warning just in time.

_____

8. The book, lost years ago, suddenly reappeared.

_____

9. To forget her troubles, Becky read an exciting novel.

_____

10. I hate eating ice cream in February. _____

11. The children took one last look at the fading sun.

_____

12. Many people's instinct is to run at the first sign of trouble.

_____

13. Hiding in the woods, Herb observed a coven of witches.

_____

14. Mr. Bullion's favorite subject is banking. _____

15. The person to watch is Felice Cortez. _____

16. Penguins, birds found in Antarctica, can't fly.

_____

17. The angry guest got up from his chair to leave.

_____

18. Fran gave sledding another try. _____

19. The Hoover High Huskies suffered a crushing defeat.

_____

20. Let me make a snowman with you, Rita. _____

H. *Directions:* Write ten sentences of your own that contain infinitives.
Then underline each infinitive and indicate at the end of the sentence
whether it is functioning as a **noun**, an **adjective**, or an **adverb**.
EXAMPLE: To travel on foot can be tiring.   noun

1. _____

2. _____

3. _____

4. _____

5. _____

6. _____

7. _____

8. _____

9. _____

10. _____

PART III. COMPREHENSIVE EXERCISES

16. DEPENDENT CLAUSES

A. *Directions:* Enclose the dependent clauses in the following sentences in parentheses. Then identify each clause by writing **adjective**, **adverb**, or **noun** in the space provided at the end of the sentence.
EXAMPLE: The boy (who spoke) is my brother. _____adjective_____

1. Your brother, whom I met yesterday, looks like you.

   _____

2. He fell when his ski broke. _____

3. When you get hungry, please fix yourself some lunch.

   _____

4. Give whoever is absent the message. _____

5. We did not see Patrick, who arrived very late.

   _____

6. We'll find whatever you lost tomorrow. _____

7. Whoever comes late will miss the show. _____

8. The store where I bought my new pants is having a sale.

   _____

9. When it rains, the traffic becomes impossible.

   _____

10. Kadem forgot the ball he brought to soccer practice.

    _____

11. Alia got upset because we lost the game. _____

12. The directions were for whoever needed them.

    _____

13. Jason ate the soup that contained fish eyes. ___

14. If it continues snowing, school will be cancelled.

    _____

15. Naomi's lunch, which she makes herself, is always the same.

    _____

16. That the field was so wet was unfortunate. _____

17. After Souyan came home, she watched television.

    _____

18. Kerry is afraid that he won't remember his lines.

    _____

19. The strategy of the game is what I enjoy most.

    _____

20. Robyn thinks her hair is too short.   _____

B. *Directions:* In the following sentences enclose the dependent clauses in parentheses. Then identify each clause by writing **adjective, adverb** or **noun** in the space provided at the end of the sentence.
   EXAMPLE: (What they said) was terribly confusing.
   _____noun_____

1. Harrow won't go unless he gets a ride.   _____

2. We interviewed people whose opinions varied greatly.

   _____

3. I'll never forget the time when I sat on a cactus.

   _____

4. You may order whatever you want for dinner.

   _____

5. Let's wait until the announcement is made. _____

6. Since Connie arrived early, I asked her for help.

   _____

7. When he comes home, tell him Josh called. _____

8. Beside the trail grew mushrooms that were poisonous.

   _____

9. Please return the video to the store before it closes.

   _____

10. My brother never agrees with what I say.   _____

11. Calvin knows I can't stand that music.   _____

12. She's the one who always needs help.   _____

13. The campsite we chose was covered with poison ivy.

    _____

14. Although it was June, it was still cold in the mountains.

    _____

15. The restaurant where we met Elbert is next to the zoo.

    _____

16. Martha can't play because she broke her arm.

    _____

17. The judges will present whoever wins a trophy.

    _____

18. Rock climbing is how Pat spends most of her free time.

    _____

19. The outlaw hid the money where no one could find it.

    _____

20. Our dog was named after the heroine of *Rigoletto*, which is our
    favorite opera. _____

C. *Directions:* Enclose each dependent clause in parentheses. Then indicate the function of each clause in the space provided at the end of the sentence.

S for subject	OP for object of the preposition
DO for direct object	ADJ for adjective
IO for indirect object	ADV for adverb
PN for predicate noun	

EXAMPLE: (As we drove), the landscape became barren.
_____ ADV _____

THE "WAR TO END ALL WARS"

1. World War I, which was fought differently from wars of the past,
   changed Europe forever. _____

2. When the war began, people everywhere were overjoyed.

   _____

3. They believed war would solve Europe's problems.

   _____

4. One major new development in World War I was that there was
   a standoff between the two sides. _____

5. Because they were so evenly matched, neither side could advance
   against the other. _____

6. The machine gun was the weapon most responsible for how the
   war was fought. _____

7. Its rapid fire of bullets, which showered the battlefields, made advancement impossible. _____

8. At Ypres, where four battles were fought, the front never shifted more than eleven miles. _____

9. The number of men who were killed at Ypres over these few miles was over a million. _____

10. For protection, soldiers dug deep trenches that stretched 475 miles across France. _____

11. The area between opposing trenches, which was called "no man's land," was sometimes only ten yards wide. _____

12. Whoever fought in the trenches spent most of his time digging. _____

13. It has been calculated that the British issued their troops over 10 million spades. _____

14. If one placed all these trenches end to end, they would reach around the world. _____

15. Since the trenches were about 8 feet deep, most were filled with water or mud. _____

16. Trenches provided whoever lived there only limited protection. _____

17. Anyone whose attention lapsed might become the target of a sniper. _____

18. Serving in the trenches was a time when soldiers were exposed to disease, poison gas, and stress. _____

19. The generals who planned the battles rarely visited the trenches. _____

20. These generals hoped bigger and bigger attacks would gain victory, but they never experienced the terrible consequences of their policies. _____

D. *Directions:* Enclose each dependent clause in parentheses. Then indicate the function of each clause in the space provided at the end of the sentence.

| S for subject | OP for object of the preposition |
| DO for direct object | ADJ for adjective |

IO for indirect object   ADV for adverb
PN for predicate noun

EXAMPLE: The movie lasted (until I went to bed.) _____ADV_____

1. As long as it's daylight, you can ride your bike.

   _____

2. I don't know whom she will ask to the dance.

   _____

3. Whatever she sings is always good. _____

4. The team whose guard is so short won the game.

   _____

5. Dave enjoys people who love the outdoors. _____

6. My cousin, whom I visited this summer, is a dancer.

   _____

7. She issued passes to whoever needed them.

   _____

8. Jamila arrived after the movie started. _____

9. Send whoever is absent a notice about the meeting.

   _____

10. He'll never make it in time unless the traffic clears.

    _____

11. Justin didn't know how the book ended.

    _____

12. Swimming is what I do best. _____

13. Although bats are harmless, people find them scary.

    _____

14. Before you go, please turn off the lights. _____

15. The seats we reserved are already taken. _____

16. Antarctica is a place where few animals can live.

    _____

17. When the sun sets in the desert, many animals begin their search
    for food. _____

18. We hiked where the ground was dry. _____

19. Nineteen sixty-eight was a year when many upsetting events oc-
    curred. _____

20. Faye told me she wasn't coming. _____

17. VERBALS

A. *Directions:* For each verb listed below, write two sentences. In one sentence use the verb as a participle; in the other sentence use the verb as a gerund. Label each participle (PART) and gerund (GER). Use separate paper for this exercise.

EXAMPLE: love

PART

The orphan needed a new home and loving parents.

GER

Loving those who care for us is easy.

1. jog	8. take	15. eat
2. ski	9. wish	16. paint
3. smell	10. stay	17. burn
4. throw	11. grow	18. cut
5. ask	12. play	19. write
6. taste	13. call	20. drive
7. listen	14. whistle	

B. *Directions:* Underline each verbal and label it **PART** for participle, **GER** for gerund, or **INF** for infinitive.

GER

EXAMPLE: Think about writing.

1. Maddie patched her worn coat.

2. She wanted to wear it to the game.

3. Riding the train can be fun.

4. The purring cat provided comfort to the small child.

5. To try hard is what counts.

6. She placed her finished book on the shelf.

7. Sue Ellen liked swimming in the pond on warm summer days.

8. The mother picked up the trembling child and placed him gently on the couch.

9. Writing can be difficult, but nothing good comes easily.

10. The senator said, "We live in trying times."

11. The instrument to play for this song is the guitar.

12. Thomas did not want to wash the dishes.

13. After completing his work, Walter watched his favorite T.V. program.
14. Every morning the ringing of his alarm clock woke Joseph.
15. Bo found the lost car keys on the bookcase.
16. Ms. Walker placed her walking stick by the door.
17. Mr. Craft encouraged his son to read the newspaper.
18. Joan signed up for cross-country running.
19. The marching band will hold practice during eighth period.
20. Ordering supplies took the storekeeper most of the morning.

C. *Directions:* Underline each verbal in the sentences below and label its type, part of speech, and function. Some sentences contain more than one verbal.

PART/ADJ

INF/N/DO

EXAMPLE: Bringing home his friend for dinner, Tom hoped to give

PART/ADJ

some companionship to his ailing sister.

1. Listening to old radio shows brought back pleasant memories to the elderly gentleman.
2. One must believe in leprechauns to see them.
3. Maud lectured on the rewinding of video tapes.
4. After spending his allowance on a prized baseball card, Alan could not afford a movie.
5. Unable to see the blackboard without her glasses, Missy missed the homework assignment.
6. Written material can be mailed fourth class.
7. Eduardo's goal is to swim the English channel.
8. Managing her father's farm gave Angela a chance to put into practice new agricultural theories.
9. Ann Marie planned to attend a student production of Thornton Wilder's *Our Town.*
10. Had you read the finished story, you would have liked it.
11. The prepared question on the test was demanding and difficult.
12. Whistling a happy tune, Stewart began to iron his shirts.
13. Oliver stopped listening to his radio.

14. Children should not spend too much time watching television.

15. The special exhibit was designed to attract large crowds.

16. Talking with his teacher, Alexander was surprised to learn that he had received an "A" on his project.

17. Saul hated cleaning his room.

18. Traveling by plane, Marc expected to arrive on time in San Francisco for the wedding.

19. Ms. Shukla called to change the meeting time.

20. Brushing your teeth after eating should help to prevent decaying teeth.

D. *Directions:* Underline each verbal in the sentences below and label its type, part of speech, and function. Some sentences contain more than one verbal.

EXAMPLE: By closely <u>examining</u> [GER/N/OP] the evidence, the detective was able <u>to deduce</u> [INF/ADV] the identity of the <u>suspected</u> [PART/ADJ] murderer.

1. The floating bobbin attracted the trout.

2. By frequently fertilizing the soil, Patrick was able to produce immense vegetables.

3. Sylvie decided to pay for the broken window out of her allowance.

4. To warm themselves, the Andersons went into the heated lodge.

5. When playing checkers, Marcus gives winning his all.

6. Diving well takes practice, as does swimming.

7. Ms. Nguyen drove the used car to test the engine.

8. The newly mown grass clung to our shoes.

9. Having eaten a package of cookies, Willie drank a glass of chilled milk.

10. It was raining on the day that we had planned to go to the lake.

11. The small boy buried his dead hamster in a battered shoebox.

12. Sakeena placed the blooming plant in the window to give it more sunshine.

13. Tom added beaten eggs to the batter before mixing it.

14. Having slept soundly all night, the child woke up ready to go to school.
15. The scrawled message was difficult to read.
16. The best tactic for seizing the other team's mascot is to take it at night.
17. Sneaking out of the house is fun to do on sparkling summer days.
18. To corner a frightened animal is often dangerous.
19. Wallace hates sitting in confined places.
20. Feeding and caring for this guinea pig will help your team to defeat the opposition.

18. FUNCTIONS OF THE NOUN

A. *Directions:* Underline the nouns and personal pronouns in the following sentences. Then label the function of each of these nouns and pronouns. Also, underline and label any predicate adjectives.

S for subject
DO for direct object
IO for indirect object
OP for object of the preposition

PN for predicate noun
APP for appositive
PA for predicate adjective

EXAMPLE: $\overset{\text{S}}{\underline{\text{Aaron}}}$ lost his $\overset{\text{DO}}{\underline{\text{compass}}}$ in the $\overset{\text{OP}}{\underline{\text{grass}}}$.

AN EGYPTIAN PHARAOH

1. The world was thrilled by the discovery of the tomb of King Tut, an Egyptian pharaoh.
2. In 1922 the archaeologist Howard Carter found this ancient grave.
3. Behind sealed doors lay rich treasures of an ancient civilization.
4. Carter unearthed many chambers of jewels and priceless artifacts.
5. After thousands of years, flowers on top of the coffin still retained their faint colors.
6. These treasures were extremely valuable to Egyptian historians.
7. They gave the world important information about the lives of ancient Egyptians.
8. Why did the Egyptian kings hoard so much wealth in their tombs?
9. Their religion taught them a belief in an afterlife.
10. Pharaohs were gods in the eyes of ancient Egyptians.
11. They would be welcomed by the other gods into the land of the dead.
12. Pharaohs believed their spirits, the *ka*, would need things for the afterlife.
13. Most of the pharaohs must have been very poor in the next world.

14. Thieves upset the royal plans and stole the valuables from the tombs.
15. They even broke into the tomb of Tutankhamen, but apparently fled empty-handed.
16. Tutankhamen was a child-king in ancient Egypt.
17. He took the throne at the age of nine.
18. Tutankhamen brought Egypt peace for ten years and then died.
19. The cause of his death is unknown.
20. Today archaeologists continue their search for tombs of the Egyptian pharaohs, but none has proved as revealing as Tutankhamen's.

B. *Directions:* Underline the nouns and personal pronouns in the following sentences. Then label the function of each of these nouns and pronouns. Also, underline and label any predicate adjectives.

S for subject	PN for predicate noun
DO for direct object	APP for appositive
IO for indirect object	PA for predicate adjective
OP for object of the preposition	

EXAMPLE:
$$\overset{\text{S}}{\underline{\text{Fred}}} \text{ took } \overset{\text{DO}}{\underline{\text{Sarah}}} \text{ to the } \overset{\text{OP}}{\underline{\text{museum}}}.$$

1. The koala bears of Australia are not really bears.
2. Wendy lent Sandy her bicycle.
3. The great variety in the plant world is almost unbelievable.
4. They gave us our worst defeat of the season.
5. The play, *Fences,* won several awards.
6. The sound of the cars kept me awake.
7. Carol invited me to lunch last Monday.
8. My uncle bought me a new violin for my birthday.
9. Friday will be the shortest day of the year.
10. My friend Diane asked him an embarrassing question.
11. Long hair becomes tangled very easily.
12. Where are you going during your summer vacation?
13. Don't tell the kids any more ghost stories.

14. Beatrice looked very happy before her trip.

15. That restaurant served us terrible food.

16. One of the fish in our aquarium chases the others.

17. The passengers remained calm after the accident.

18. Our guest is an author of several books about snakes.

19. The river flooded the fields along the shore.

20. A persuasive speaker, Bob won the argument easily.

19. PARTS OF SPEECH

A. *Directions:* Label the part of speech of every word in the following sentences. If a noun or pronoun functions as either an adjective or adverb, label it according to its function. You do not have to label articles.

N for noun	ADV for adverb
PRO for pronoun	PREP for preposition
V for verb	CONJ for conjunction
ADJ for adjective	INT for interjection

```
              V   PRO  V   ADJ   N      ADV
EXAMPLE: Did you cut your hair yesterday?
```

BEETHOVEN

1. Ludwig van Beethoven was born in Germany in 1770.
2. His compositions radically transformed many musical forms.
3. Alas! Beethoven's life was always a struggle.
4. His father, Johann, was a mediocre musician with a weak voice.
5. Beethoven's mother was quiet and affectionate.
6. Johann exploited his son's talents but never made much money from them.
7. Unlike Mozart, Beethoven was no prodigy and developed slowly as a musician.
8. In 1787 he went to Vienna and briefly took piano lessons from Mozart.
9. The death of his mother forced his return home.
10. By now he had become an accomplished pianist and composer.
11. At home, however, things did not go well for Beethoven.
12. He now became responsible for his family.
13. In 1792 he moved permanently to Vienna with his two brothers.
14. Beethoven soon developed problems with his hearing.
15. Oh! He knew there would be no cure for his deafness, but he gained musically from this disability.
16. He turned inward and created a new kind of music.

17. The first fruit of this change came with his Third Symphony, the *Eroica*.

18. It was vastly different from the music of the past.

19. This symphony was infinitely more powerful and expressive.

20. It was the dawn of a new age in music.

B. *Directions:* Label the part of speech of every word in the following sentences. If a noun or pronoun functions as either an adjective or adverb, label it according to its function. You do not have to label articles.

N for noun	ADV for adverb
PRO for pronoun	PREP for preposition
V for verb	CONJ for conjunction
ADJ for adjective	INT for interjection

```
      PRO   V           N   CONJ  V  PRO
EXAMPLE: I dropped the glass and broke it.
```

1. Louis almost caught a ball at the baseball game.

2. The path was muddy and slippery.

3. How did you ever get there in time?

4. He searched frantically for the telephone number.

5. Alethea went either to the library or to the lab.

6. The tank was first used during World War I.

7. My favorite music is reggae.

8. Oops! Sidra dropped her tray, but nothing broke.

9. Alexa always handles the animals carefully.

10. I should not put so much salt on my food.

C. *Directions:* Label the part of speech of every word in the following sentences. If a noun or pronoun functions as either an adjective or adverb, label it according to its function. You do not have to label articles.

N for noun	ADV for adverb
PRO for pronoun	PREP for preposition
V for verb	CONJ for conjunction
ADJ for adjective	INT for interjection

EXAMPLE: I lost my wallet and keys on the trip.

BIRDS OF PREY

1. Birds of prey come in a wide range of sizes and shapes.
2. Most of them are falcons, eagles, hawks, and vultures, but some owls are included.
3. The smallest bird of prey weighs about one ounce and is almost six inches long.
4. The largest one, the Andean condor, has a wing span of ten feet.
5. Members of this group of birds live on every continent.
6. Unfortunately, many birds of prey are endangered.
7. Some farmers shoot and trap them, yet these birds kill very few farm animals.
8. Pesticides are another great danger to the birds.
9. The increase in the human population has also caused destruction of their habitats.
10. Zoos and other organizations breed endangered birds of prey and may save them from extinction.

20. SENTENCE COMBINING

A. *Directions:* Each of the following problems contains two sentences. Using a dependent clause, combine these sentences into one sentence. Label the type of dependent clause you use either **ADJ** for adjective, **ADV** for adverb, or **N** for noun. Be sure to think about the sense of each sentence and the relationship between sentences before combining them.

EXAMPLE: I brush my teeth.
        I go to bed.

           ADV
        (After I brush my teeth,) I go to bed.

1. The Arables went to the county fair.
   Fern bought cotton candy and popcorn.

   _____

   _____

2. Buddy Holly was one of early rock and roll's most famous acts.
   He was killed in a plane crash in 1959.

   _____

   _____

3. Mr. Monty Terry was found shot in the library of his palatial home.
   He was the world's richest bachelor.

   _____

   _____

4. Ms. Kookie Krum was the prime suspect.
   Detective Miles Spade knew she hadn't committed the crime.

   _____

   _____

5. Chip did not pass in his homework on time.
   He will have to attend detention after school.

   _____

   _____

6. Colonel Peacock's alibi was confirmed by the janitor.
   He was with his niece at the time of the murder.

   _____

   _____

7. Myra arrived at the doctor's office on time for her appointment. The doctor could see her immediately.

_____

_____

8. Daniel barbecued the chicken.
Henry made the salad.

_____

_____

9. Leonard could not see the blackboard from the back of the classroom.
He went to the eye doctor to have his eyes checked.

_____

_____

10. The detective had a theory.
The butler didn't do it.

_____

_____

11. Mark Twain wrote *The Adventures of Huckleberry Finn*.
Mark Twain's real name was Samuel Clemens.

_____

_____

12. Ms. Pennymoney, secretary to Mr. Terry, gave her story to the detective.
Mr. Terry had hired her only the day before his murder.

_____

_____

13. Mr. Terry had changed his will that day.
Spade knew that.

_____

_____

14. Lucy went walking.
She took her dog with her.

_____

_____

15. Ms. Kookie Krum had helped Mr. Terry with his stamp collection.
Mr. Terry had asked her to marry him.

_____

_____

16. She was to inherit only his stamp collection.
    Someone else was to inherit the vast estate.

    _____

    _____

17. Who is that person?
    He or she must be the killer.

    _____

    _____

18. Miles Spade began to put the pieces together.
    He found the monogrammed money clip.

    _____

    _____

19. Ms. Pennymoney appeared meek and gentle.
    She was not as she appeared.

    _____

    _____

20. She was really Terry Terry, the long lost half-sister of Monty, and
    was to inherit everything.
    She had killed Monty in order to be able to pay off her bingo
    debts.

    _____

    _____

B. *Directions:* Each of the problems below contains two or more sentences.
   Using a dependent clause, combine these sentences into one sentence.
   Label the type of dependent clause that you use either **ADJ** for adjective, **ADV** for adverb or **N** for noun. Be sure to think about the
   sense of the sentence and the relationship between sentences before
   combining them.
   EXAMPLE: Mow the grass.
            Rake up the clippings.

                        ADV
            (After you mow the grass,) rake up the clippings.

1. Please give Mr. Elias the packages.
   He is going to the post office this afternoon.

   _____

   _____

2. Lulu was going to the party.
   She carefully washed her dress.

   _____

   _____

3. With this humid weather, heavy fog may form overnight.
   If so, driving will be dangerous.

   _____

   _____

4. The English town of Stratford-on-Avon is flooded each year
   with tourists from all over the world.
   Shakespeare was born there.

   _____

   _____

5. Drive carefully on the narrow, twisting road.
   You may have an accident.

   _____

   _____

6. Wet the car down thoroughly.
   Wash it well with soapy water and a sponge.

   _____

   _____

7. The book was put away.
   We do not know where.

   _____

   _____

8. Loch Ness is the largest fresh water lake in Great Britain.
   It is known best for its supposed inhabitant, the Loch Ness Monster.

   _____

   _____

9. John Adams began his career as a farmer and a country lawyer.
   Later he was to travel as an American diplomat throughout Europe.

   _____

   _____

10. Ms. Kawasaki read the review about the film in the newspaper.
    She decided not to see the film.

    _____

    _____

11. Katherine Mansfield was born in Australia.
    She is one of the world's best-known short story writers.
    She lived most of her adult life in England.

    _____

    _____

12. The principal made an announcement over the loud speaker.
    The basketball game had been cancelled.

    _____

    _____

13. Six-month-old babies put everything into their mouths.
    Mothers and fathers know this.

    _____

    _____

14. The green tips of the tulips poked through the earth.
    This told us spring was coming.

    _____

    _____

15. It came in the mail last week.
    I had forgotten to open the letter from my aunt.

    _____

    _____

16. DNA's structure is similar to a corkscrew.
    This fact was discovered by Francis Crick and James Watson.

    _____

    _____

17. Women made pieced quilts from many tiny bits of material.
    These women wasted nothing.

    _____

    _____

18. Isaac Merrit Singer got a patent for the sewing machine.
    He was born in 1811.
    The sewing machine revolutionized home and industrial sewing.

    _____

    _____

19. A sinkhole is a natural hole in the land.
This natural depression connects with an underground passage.
Sinkholes are usually found in limestone regions.

_____

_____

20. She was fined and her library card revoked.
She had kept the library books long past the due date.

_____

_____

C. *Directions:* Each of the following problems contains two or more sentences. Using a semicolon, a colon, an appositive, a conjunction, a verbal, or a dependent clause, combine these sentences into one sentence. Be sure to think about the sense of the sentence and the relationship between sentences before combining them.
EXAMPLE: My aunt will visit us.
She is coming for Christmas.

My aunt will visit us for Christmas.

1. It began to rain hard.
The game was called during the seventh inning.

_____

_____

2. Tomorrow the science class will go to the Museum of Science.
The students will go to see the planetarium show.
It is a show about meteors.

_____

_____

3. Washington Irving wrote *Rip Van Winkle.*
It is a story about a lazy man.
He slept for twenty years.

_____

_____

4. Estrella liked to ski.
She took lessons.
She learned to snow plow.

_____

_____

5. My mother had a long list of errands for me to do.
She wanted me to drop off the books at the library, pick up a chair at the repair shop, get gas in the car, go to the garage sale, and pick up my dad at work.

_____

_____

6. Tests trouble many students.
They often feel flustered.

_____

_____

7. Joshua drove by.
He saw his friend.
His friend was waiting at the bus stop.
Joshua offered him a ride to school.

_____

_____

8. Delia blew out the candles on her cake.
She made two wishes.
She wished for a horse.
She wished for a saddle.

_____

_____

9. You may go anywhere.
I will always follow.

_____

_____

10. Mr. Cleaver slept more than eight hours.
He still felt tired.

_____

_____

11. You said you would help file the newspaper clippings.
You did not.
You said you would crop the pictures.
You did not.

_____

_____

12. Patty measured the height of the bookcase.
Then she measured the width.
Then she measured the length.

Afterwards she marked the lumber.
Then she sawed the lumber.

_____

_____

13. Andy helped his sister with her homework.
    This always made him feel proud.

    _____

    _____

14. Mitch did not take his shoes to the cobbler.
    He had to wear his blue high-top sneakers to the dance.

    _____

    _____

15. You are coming to my house after school.
    Bring my knapsack with you.
    It is the one with the patch on the front.

    _____

    _____

16. Blacks had boycotted bus companies before the successful boycott
    of 1954 in Montgomery, Alabama.
    These boycotts were unsuccessful.
    Bus companies would not ban segregated seating.

    _____

    _____

17. Virginia Woolf was the daughter of a well-known writer.
    He was Leslie Stephen.
    She married a well-known writer.
    He was Leonard Woolf.

    _____

    _____

18. Wyoming Territory enfranchised women in 1869.
    It was the first government in the world to grant women the right
    to vote.

    _____

    _____

19. Mrs. Parker went roller skating.
    She put on her elbow and knee pads and her helmet.
    She skated on the asphalt path in the park.

    _____

    _____

20. Rita Dove won the Pulitzer Prize.
    She writes poetry.

    _____

    _____

D. *Directions:* Each of the problems below contains two or more sentences. Using a semicolon, a colon, an appositive, a conjunction, a verbal, or a dependent clause, combine these sentences into one sentence. Be sure to think about the sense of the sentence and the relationship between sentences before combining them.

   EXAMPLE: The snow fell to a depth of three feet.
            Schools and businesses were closed.

            Falling to a depth of three feet, snow closed schools and businesses.

SEA SERPENTS

1. There have always been tales of sea serpents.
   Both landlubbers and sailors enjoy them.

   _____

   _____

2. In 1734 a missionary wrote about seeing a sea serpent.
   The missionary's name was Hans Egede.
   He saw the sea serpent on his way to Greenland.

   _____

   _____

3. Edege wrote that the monster was large.
   It was as tall as the masthead of his ship.
   It was three times the length of the ship.
   Its skin was covered with scales.

   _____

   _____

4. Like Edege's sighting, many of the early sightings occurred in colder waters.
   In the 19th century sightings became more widely reported.

   _____

   _____

5. One of the most famous sightings occurred in 1848.
   It is the sighting of the "Daedalus sea monster."
   It was reported by the sailors of the *H.M.S. Daedalus*.

   _____

   _____

6. The British admiralty required a report of the sighting.
   The report is part of the official record.
   That fact is what makes this sighting so unusual.

   _____

   _____

7. The captain gave the report.
   He was considered trustworthy.
   His report was confirmed by the other men aboard the *Daedalus*.

   _____

   _____

8. The report described a serpent.
   The serpent kept its head and shoulders above the sea.
   The creature was brown.
   It had a head like a snake.
   It had a mane.

   _____

   _____

9. In the twentieth century interest in sea serpents dropped.
   There were few sightings.

   _____

   _____

10. The last reported sighting was in 1915.
    The sighting was made by a U-boat captain.
    He states that he killed a sea serpent.

    _____

    _____

11. A German U-boat was on patrol.
    It sank a British steamer.
    The steamer was called *Iberian*.

    _____

    _____

12. The steamer sank.
    There was an explosion.
    Something was thrown to the surface.
    It was a wildly thrashing sea serpent.

    _____

    _____

13. The U-boat captain described the creature.
    It was sixty feet long.
    It looked like a crocodile.

    _____

    _____

14. Recently there have been no sightings.
    In 1969 there was evidence of another type.

    _____

    _____

15. A shrimp boat was patrolling in the Shelikof Strait.
    The Shelikof Strait is located between the Alaska peninsula and
    the Kodiak Islands.
    The boat picked up a strange shape on its echo sounder.

    _____

    _____

16. The tracing on the echo sounder looked like a plesiosaurus.
    A plesiosaurus is a kind of dinosaur.

    _____

    _____

17. The echo sounder was examined for malfunctions.
    The company which made the echo sounder examined it.

    _____

    _____

18. The company believed the tracing had been forged.
    The cryptozoologist disagreed.
    The cryptozoologist was Ivan Sanderson.
    A cryptozoologist is a person who studies the evidence for signs
    of unknown animals.

    _____

    _____

19. The seas are more travelled.
    We have no other evidence.

    _____

    _____

20. A sea serpent has never been washed on shore.
    There has never been a photograph.

    _____

    _____

21. PUNCTUATION

A. *Directions:* In the following sentences decide whether each adjective clause is essential or non-essential and then place commas around non-essential adjective clauses.

EXAMPLE: She is the candidate who should win the primary.
Mr. Kearney, who teaches Latin, proctored the study hall.

1. Games that are played on grass cannot be played in snow.
2. Charles whom you met at the mall is my father.
3. Animals that have four stomachs regurgitate their food.
4. Television programs that portray excessive violence often give viewers an unreal picture of the world.
5. Bulbs that bloom in spring must be planted in the fall.
6. The trophy which the team won in the tournament is in the trophy case.
7. The Shakers who invented many household items were a religious group.
8. We gave our used books to people who needed them.
9. Cars that have smaller engines get better gas mileage.
10. A name that now stands for traitor is quisling.
11. My coach said that marathoners who eat pasta on the night before the race have more stamina.
12. The English who are famous for their love of tea are often accused of being reserved.
13. The cereal which contained both oat and wheat flakes became soggy in milk.
14. According to Aristotle, a tragedy is a play that evokes pity and fear in the audience.
15. June's baby who can crawl often gets into a great deal of mischief.
16. Ms. Jimenez gave me an African violet that blooms profusely every March.
17. Hamlet which Shakespeare wrote is a great play.
18. The cow that just had a calf stands under the tree.

19. A tetrahedron is a geometric three-dimensional shape that has four sides.

20. My mother never liked those days on which she had to get up in the dark.

B. *Directions:* Each of the following sentences contains at least one error in punctuation. Rewrite each sentence correctly in the space provided.

EXAMPLE: Since you can t come we will send you a tape of the meeting!
Since you can't come, we will send you a tape of the meeting.

1. Monopoly which has street names from actual streets found in Atlantic City New Jersey is fun to play.

   _____

2. The coronation of King George V was the first public ceremony carried on live television in Great Britain!

   _____

3. My English teacher who reads aloud to us often takes us to the library.

   _____

4. The Johnson's house is located at the corner of Elm Street and Fourth Avenue.

   _____

5. One of the countries, that makes up North America, is Canada.

   _____

6. Mrs. Coombs yelled, 'Stop that. Youre going to break it.'

   _____

7. Students, who study hard, hand in work on time and read beyond the assignment, usually receive higher grades.

   _____

8. Whenever Mr. Granada comes into the classroom he asks who's absent?

   _____

9. The book *Ishi* which is about the last Yahi Indian in California was written by an anthropologist.

   _____

10. The time, during which Queen Victoria ruled, is the Victorian Era.

_____

11. When I left for school the clock in the kitchen read 8;15.

_____

12. Martys swimming has improved greatly, since he started lessons at the Boys Club.

_____

13. Neither you nor I am going to win." said Carla.

_____

14. Dawn began the letter "Dear Sir;" when she wrote to the editor of "The Boston Globe."

_____

15. I didn't make an appointment with the dentist, however, Im sure Dr Gibson will see me for an emergency.

_____

16. When Jared put on his fathers' suit he looked silly but he wanted to wear it any way.

_____

17. Having arrived at the lake Margaret took her fishing pole, and began to cast for fish.

_____

18. Mrs Metcalf asked, "whether we had enjoyed the movie?"

_____

19. We hadnt added baking powder, consequently the biscuits were flat, and hard.

_____

20. For the service Andy chose to read _Ruth 2;16._

_____

C. _Directions:_ Insert the correct punctuation where it is needed in the following sentences. You may add _'s_ when necessary.
   EXAMPLE: John said, "Let's go to the dance."

   1. Jose likes three kinds of fruit apples oranges and grapes
   2. Lucy doesnt like Jims aunt nevertheless she is always polite to her

3. Why dont you like purple mashed potatoes Ronnie asked

4. When Heather first looked out the window she couldnt see Charles car

5. Curt bought a car he paid with cash

6. Yes Sabrina the girls soccer team lost another game

7. Darn Our new paper girl Cindy is late again

8. Hurrying to catch the bus Mr Finkley fell into a puddle

9. Were going out to catch fireflies after dinner Jerome said

10. Paris which is the capital of France is a beautiful city

11. Ill go to the game Beulah however I wont enjoy it

12. Carmine asked if I was afraid of elevators but I told her I wasnt

13. Since I cant eat dairy products I never have ice cream

14. Stop that thief Harold screamed at the top of his lungs

15. Sitting in a chair in her bedroom Rosa read The Listeners a poem by Walter De la Mare

16. The book that I was reading yesterday belongs to Mrs Phillips mother

17. Alice Walker who wrote *The Color Purple* is a gifted writer said Mr Talbert my English teacher

18. Although Ive never eaten yams I dont like them but my father says I should give them a chance

19. Choose one of the following flavors strawberry chocolate or vanilla

20. I love orange soda Horace announced and I always will

22. FUNCTIONS OF WORDS, PHRASES, AND CLAUSES

A. *Directions:* Above each underlined word, phrase, or clause write its function (how it is used in the sentence).

PREP   DO

EXAMPLE: <u>Despite</u> her friend's objections, Penny decided <u>to join</u> the

ADJ

<u>debating</u> club.

THE DAY THE SKY DARKENED

1. Settlers on the Kansas frontier <u>were prepared</u> to face the usual hardships of blizzards, raiding Indians, disease, drought, and famine, but <u>nothing</u> had prepared them <u>for</u> the grasshopper plague of 1874.

2. On August 1, 1874, a peculiar white cloud <u>almost</u> hid the <u>sun.</u>

3. <u>Dropping</u> down on the fields, the cloud revealed itself to be hoards of <u>grasshoppers.</u>

4. One eyewitness said that they hit the <u>ground</u> so hard that they sounded <u>like hail.</u>

5. The grasshoppers covered the ground and everything on it <u>to a depth</u> of four inches; their weight bent corn stalks and snapped <u>tree</u> limbs.

6. <u>Ravenous,</u> the grasshoppers ate everything in <u>their</u> way.

7. Frightened settlers ran from their homes <u>to cover</u> vegetable gardens with quilts, gunny sacks, and clothing, but their efforts were <u>useless.</u>

8. The <u>grasshoppers</u> ate the <u>coverings</u> as well as the crops.

9. <u>Leaving</u> nothing but the <u>toughest</u> part of the stalks, the insects wiped out entire corn fields in a matter of minutes.

10. Trees <u>were stripped</u> of leaves and <u>fruit.</u>

11. <u>Having devoured</u> the crops, the grasshoppers invaded homes and barns, <u>where they attacked food supplies stored in cupboards, barrels, and bins.</u>

12. They also ate anything <u>made</u> of wood such as furniture, kitchen utensils, fence boards, and <u>sometimes</u> the wooden siding on cabins.

13. <u>Clothing</u> was devoured while <u>being worn</u>.

14. One woman later remembered <u>wearing</u> a white- and green-striped dress, and <u>when the grasshoppers settled on her,</u> they ate every green stripe but left the white ones.

15. Grasshoppers totally <u>covered</u> cattle and small <u>children.</u>

16. Trains could not move, <u>for</u> the tracks <u>were slick</u> with the crushed insects.

17. <u>By the</u> time the <u>plague had passed,</u> settlers had lost homes and livelihoods.

18. Even what remained was polluted; poultry and hogs had gorged themselves <u>on the insects</u>, and when slaughtered, they tasted so <u>strongly</u> of the hideous insects that people could <u>not</u> eat them.

19. All open water was unfit for <u>drinking</u> <u>because the grasshopper droppings had contaminated it.</u>

20. <u>Many</u> disheartened settlers left, but <u>many</u> stayed with hopes of future prosperity.

B. *Directions:* Above each underlined word, phrase, or clause write its function (how it is used in the sentence).

ADV   PA ADV

EXAMPLE: <u>Without help</u> Mark was <u>unable</u> <u>to complete</u> his algebra assignment.

BEATRIX POTTER: AUTHOR AND NATURALIST

1. Helen Beatrix Potter, <u>born</u> on July 28, 1866, grew up <u>in a new and prosperous section</u> of London.

2. <u>Downstairs</u> her parents lived a life of precise and punctual routine, <u>while upstairs in the nursery Beatrix lived a life of isolation and seclusion.</u>

3. She was not <u>lonely</u>, as she was able <u>to fill</u> the hours with her fantasies and studies.

4. <u>Drawing</u> animals and natural history gave <u>her</u> much pleasure.

5. On summer holidays she and her brother, <u>Bertram,</u> brought home all of the plants, animals, and insects <u>that they could find</u> and often skinned dead animals.

6. Drawing each <u>specimen</u>, Beatrix filled dozens <u>of sketch books.</u>

7. In her teens she <u>began collecting</u> live animals and at various times gave <u>shelter</u> to rabbits, bats, mice, rats, birds, lizards, newts, toads, and even a hedgehog.

8. From the specimens she learned much <u>information that challenged or added to accepted theories.</u>

9. By carefully <u>watching</u> her hedgehog hibernate, she concluded that hibernation was <u>not</u> a state caused by low temperature but was a state <u>totally</u> under the animal's control.

10. From her intense study of fungus, she wrote a paper about the spores of mold, and her <u>findings</u> were read before a <u>well-known</u> botanical group in London.

11. She <u>continued</u> <u>to study</u> natural history at the British Museum of Natural History.

12. <u>Desiring</u> scientific accuracy, most of her sketches were exact, <u>but</u> occasionally a newt in a muffler or a rabbit <u>in a bonnet</u> appeared.

13. <u>From these fantasies</u> came her next, most well-known <u>career,</u> that of a writer of children's stories.

14. At the age of twenty-six, <u>she</u> began <u>to write</u> picture letters to the children <u>of</u> a former governess.

15. A small rabbit <u>named</u> Peter made <u>his</u> first appearance in one of these letters.

16. Ten years later, in 1901, she privately published 250 <u>copies</u> of Peter's adventures <u>in Farmer MacGregor's garden.</u>

17. <u>When a publisher noticed her story and decided to publish it,</u> Beatrix said he could only <u>if the published book be small enough for the hands of a child to hold.</u>

18. For the next twenty years Beatrix Potter published <u>over</u> thirty books for children, many of <u>them</u> illustrated with drawings of her beloved Lake District.

19. With the money <u>that she earned,</u> she began her third career when she bought a farm in <u>the</u> Lake District and then married at the <u>age</u> of fifty.

20. From then on, and <u>until her death</u> at the age of seventy-seven, she was a <u>farmer</u> who spent her time in the garden, perhaps thinking of herself as Mrs. MacGregor.

23. ERRORS

Directions: Each sentence below contains at least one error. Rewrite each sentence correctly in the space provided.

EXAMPLE: Him playing first base in todays game makes no sense?
His playing first base in today's game makes no sense.

1. Its clear to me that first we must measure the chemical, then we must heat it.

2. As you see the foundation to the house has suffered no damage.

3. Either he or I am supposed to go to visit the Websters but we havent decided which one will go.

4. Make sure to read John Keats "Ode To A Nightingale" before tomorrow.

5. The sportscaster reported the scores for the basketball, hockey and football games then he showed the highlights from each game.

6. When we met the french consul we asked him questions about France's main exports.

7. The most important source for this report is *New Wave* 4.12!

8. Your not the only one whose early.

9. The report looked badly with the smudges all over it's title page.

10. Because my report is due on monday, I asked my History teacher for help.

11. The team members and the coach helps at a soup kitchen on saturdays.

12. The Lincoln memorial is one of the sights in Washington D.C.

13. The pen that he have in his pocket leaks.

_____

14. My uncle playing soccer is the funniest sight Ive ever seen.

_____

15. This stew tastes funnily, Warren must have forgotten to put in the seasonings.

_____

16. Elizabeth II is the first queen to rule Great Britain, since queen Victoria died.

_____

17. However you play this game youre practice will pay off.

_____

18. The lights shone brightly the actress played the scene.

_____

19. Where did you go last night:" asked Stevie?

_____

20. Where you land a plane, is important to the people, who ride with you.

_____

Directions: Each sentence below contains at least one error. Rewrite each sentence correctly in the space provided.

EXAMPLE: Its me calling during dinner that her father doesnt like.

It's my calling during dinner that her father doesn't like.

1. My uncle, Dan, visits my mother every Veterans Day.

_____

2. The participant in the pie eating contest Mrs. Quimbly had to eat all the pies?

_____

3. Does you think that well see a comet tonight?

_____

4. The janitor always asks us, "to pick up our milk cartons."

_____

5. Salvatore liked to read after "lights out" other campers tried to get some sleep.

_____

6. My black cat Dracula enjoys halloween more than any other holiday.

_____

7. My family has relatives in Missouri, Kansas and nebraska!

_____

8. Has Mr. Owen and Ms. Ashanta arrived or dont you know.

_____

9. Where is the cattle that we were going to herd?

_____

10. One of my brothers, Hank, come home from College every weekend.

_____

11. I thought her coming late was suspicious?

_____

12. Eureka, Ive discovered the solution to the algebra problem.

_____

13. Using a computer, makes work, that once took hours, go much faster.

_____

14. Has you read *The Art of Doublespeak* in this months "Lost Language"?

_____

15. The jury's decision were reached soon after it left the courtroom.

_____

16. All of the trucks, but my fathers, has had new brakes.

_____

17. He are one of those people who likes rock and roll music.

_____

18. Chasing the cat, a banana peel tripped Harry.

_____

19. When will you see the new exhibit, maybe you don't want to see it?

_____

20. However you complete the assignment it is due on monday, June 8, 1998.

_____